THE BOOK THAT BRIDGES THE GAP BETWEEN *KNOWING* AND *DOING*!

As an executive, you *know* that in today's business world your company needs every advantage it can seize. It has to position itself exactly in terms of consumer demand. It has to carefully calculate not only its own moves but those of its competition. It has to squarely face its own deficiencies and continually upgrade its product and the performance of its people. In short, it has to achieve an effective blending of old-fashioned selling and contemporary utilization of corporate culture, short-term solutions and long-term strategies, to attain the bottom-line results that are the ultimate proof of excellence.

You know it—and now this book helps you *do* it for your company and yourself.

THE WORKBOOK FOR CREATING EXCELLENCE

CRAIG R. HICKMAN is Chairman of Management Perspectives Group, an innovative executive development firm, and serves as a special adviser to Arthur Young International's Strategic Management Consulting Service. A Harvard M.B.A., he lectures and conducts workshops for major corporations such as Frito-Lay, Amoco, and AT&T.

MICHAEL A. SILVA is CEO of Bennett Enterprises, a 100-year-old company specializing in mergers and acquisitions with particular emphasis on Japanese-American joint ventures. A popular speaker to executive groups, he has addressed the executives of over a hundred Fortune 500 firms during the past two years.

Mr. Hickman and Mr. Silva are co-authors of the best-selling *Creating Excellence*.

THE WORKBOOK FOR CREATING EXCELLENCE

by Craig R. Hickman
and Michael A. Silva

A PLUME BOOK

NEW AMERICAN LIBRARY

NEW YORK AND SCARBOROUGH, ONTARIO

DEDICATION

*To the men and women
who strive every day to create
excellence in their organizations*

Copyright © 1986 by Craig R. Hickman
and Michael A. Silva

 PLUME TRADEMARK REG. U.S. PAT. OFF. AND FOREIGN COUNTRIES
REG. TRADEMARK—MARCA REGISTRADA
HECHO EN HARRISONBURG, VA., U.S.A.

SIGNET, SIGNET CLASSIC, MENTOR, PLUME,
MERIDIAN and NAL BOOKS are published *in the
United States* by New American Library, 1633
Broadway, New York, New York 10019, *in Canada*
by The New American Library of Canada Limited,
81 Mack Avenue, Scarborough, Ontario M1L 1M8

Library of Congress Cataloging-in-Publication Data

Hickman, Craig R.
    The workbook for creating excellence.

    1. Management.   I. Silva, Michael A., 1951–
II. Hickman, Craig R. Creating excellence.   III. Title.
HD31.H4816   1986   658.4   85-21670
ISBN 0-452-25749-2

First Printing, March, 1986

1   2   3   4   5   6   7   8   9

PRINTED IN THE UNITED STATES OF AMERICA

ACKNOWLEDGMENTS

*We owe a great debt to the readers who
responded so enthusiastically to our first book,
Creating Excellence: Managing Corporate
Culture, Strategy, and Change in the New Age.
Their responses pleased us not just because they
found our advice useful, but because their
thoughtful observations and questions
underscored the fact that thousands of
managers are working tirelessly to improve the
quality and productivity of their companies. We
have learned a lot from them, and in an effort
to make our advice even more useful, we have
addressed many of their concerns in this
present book.*

*In addition, we must thank the team whose
efforts have made this book possible. Our
friend and literary agent, Michael Snell, once
again helped develop and write the text,
constantly challenging us to refine and clarify
our ideas. At New American Library, Arnold
Dolin and Jill Grossman continued to support
us with enthusiasm and good advice, and in Salt
Lake City our assistants, Dixie Clark and Mary
Kowalczyk, spent long hours at the word
processor, while our research assistant,
Marcello Hunter, provided valuable
background information.*

*Most authors express appreciation for the
patience and understanding of their families,
but no words can capture the gratitude we feel
for the support we have received during our
work on this project. All managers should be
blessed with such safe harbors.*

CONTENTS

CHAPTER 10

TYPE B ORGANIZATIONS 219

CHAPTER 11

TYPE A ORGANIZATIONS 239

INTRODUCTION

In 1969 Fred Borch, then CEO of General Electric Company, hired the consulting firm McKinsey & Company to overhaul GE's planning activities, and McKinsey's results helped foster American business's decade-long fascination with formal strategic planning. Throughout the 1970s, major business schools churned out an army of MBAs equipped with all the complex tools of this new "science." Unfortunately, these technocrats took important planning decisions out of the hands of line managers, a turn of events that at least partially accounts for the much-lamented decline in American productivity.

McKinsey itself soon saw that its own initially useful work had been taken to alarming extremes. In the words of Frederick Gluck, a McKinsey director, "It was a search for shortcuts. It took the *thinking* out of what you have to do to be competitively successful in the future." Worse, the strategists practiced a sort of "neutron bomb" approach: matrices and models and organizational structures survived, but the people were obliterated. More than one company ended up regretting that it had placed too much faith in the strategy fad:

- Lone Star Industries thought it had fabricated a fail-safe strategy when it decided to focus exclusively on its cement-related businesses and sell any endeavor that compromised this focus. The strategy, based on an anticipated cement shortage, seemed sound enough, but the shortage failed to materialize. Having geared its whole strategy to exploit high prices, Lone Star found itself unable to compete effectively against low-cost producers.
- Oak Industries adopted a strategy to diversify into subscription TV and cable TV equipment, a major opportunity Oak Industries thought itself well positioned to seize. However, Oak badly underestimated the strength and resolve of its competition and did not keep up with TV equipment developments. As a result the strategy failed.
- Trailways hit upon a two-pronged strategy to ensure its survival in the bus business: creation of strong alliances with independent bus companies and persuasion of industry regulators to hold Greyhound's market share to 67 percent in intercity markets. This seemingly brilliant strategy fell apart when deregulation hit the industry and Greyhound's own price war rendered alliances with independents meaningless.

With the realization that strategy had run amok came a new battalion of authors and consultants promising a whole new set of surefire cures: Japanese-style techniques, stronger corporate cultures, and a renewed emphasis on the so-called soft people skills. Despite offering some important insights, this new breed stressed the cultural aspects of management without paying sufficient attention to strategic thinking. As a result, the culture craze started out at the same stage of development as the strategy-planning fad was in the early 1970s.

Although many critics have already begun to assail the new-style culture building as just another cynical and manipulative technique, we insist that executives can create beneficial cultures, provided they build them upon a deep and honest caring for the welfare of people. However, culture building requires a major investment of time, money, and energy and cannot succeed as a quick fix for what ails an organization. A number of companies have learned this lesson the hard way:

- Adolph Coors, longing to become a national force in the beer industry, hoped it could merely order its strong quality-oriented culture to become more marketing oriented, but when the company employed a new strategy that required such a major shift in culture it could not compete successfully with Miller and Bud. Why? Because strategies that require immediate shifts in culture always come up short.
- Western Union Corporation, recognizing a need to change its slow-moving, bureaucratic culture, developed after years of operating in regulated industries, tried to quickly force its people into alien business environments: long-distance phone service, gift ordering by phone, pay phones in commercial airplanes, and so on. It's not surprising that the company's performance in these new businesses has been dismal. The company's management simply hasn't been able to mold its people into marketing entrepreneurs overnight.
- Napco Industries, a non-food distributor to grocery stores, set its sights on dominating the distribution business nationwide, but it saddled its healthy culture with ill-advised acquisitions and logistical problems associated with a "too aggressive" nationwide expansion of its distribution network that the culture couldn't handle.

All these cases illustrate the fact that no matter how brilliant your strategy, it will not succeed unless a strong, congruent corporate culture implements it; and no matter how strong your culture, it will not create excellence unless you marshal it behind a brilliant, congruent strategy. To assist you in developing your own durable strategy-culture alloy in an ever more complex and rapidly changing marketplace, we have developed a proven program that will help you thoroughly analyze, then adjust your own organizational situation.

Today's managers face the awesome task of becoming simultaneously strategic thinkers and culture builders, always forging the twin components of excellence into strong yet flexible alloys. In our book *Creating Excellence: Managing Corporate Culture, Strategy, and Change in the New Age*, we showed executives how to balance strategy and culture with six New Age skills: insight, sensitivity, vision, versatility, focus, and patience.

Our goal with *The Workbook for Creating Excellence* is to arm you with the practical tools you need to tap the full power of your unique strategy-culture alloy. Therefore, we have designed this workbook to thoroughly apply the lessons of our first book, providing you with a step-by-step program that can help you master both strategic thinking and culture building.

No matter what your business, and regardless of your present organizational structure, you must always consider the six fundamental factors on which lasting excellence depends:

- Satisfying customer needs
- Sustaining competitive advantage
- Capitalizing on company strengths
- Cultivating a commitment to a common purpose
- Developing competence to deliver superior performance
- Perpetuating consistency in commitment and competence

The first three factors form the basis of any successful strategy, while the last three provide the key ingredients of any strong culture. In Chapters 1 through 6 of this workbook you will be considering each of these factors separately, but you must keep reminding yourself that in a dynamic organization each factor constantly affects, and is affected by, the others. As you work your way through Part I, keep in mind the fact that consideration of just one factor at a time does not adequately reflect the complexity of corporate development in the real world.

Throughout the workbook, and particularly in Part I, we stress *thought processes* as the key to success, because we believe businesspeople must develop new and improved mental skills to cope with the complexities of a changing world.

Many students of contemporary business have called the 1980s the age of the entrepreneur, but, in fact, the history of American business is really the history of innovation. In an effort to harness innovation within the corporate walls, many executives have tried to instill an entrepreneurial spirit within their organizations. However, executives themselves must become innovators, imaginatively and creatively solving the problems that always come with change. Earlier we called such innovative managers New Age executives, but occasionally in this workbook you will encounter a new name for them, the *execupreneurs*. By execupreneur we simply mean a leader who has mastered the ability to constantly and simultaneously manage both strategy and culture in a world of accelerated, constant change. To help you become an execupreneur, we have constructed for each chapter in Part I a hypothetical organization you can follow through the exercises before you formulate your answers. These sophisticated yet easy-to-follow exercises guide you step by step through a detailed assessment of the strategy-culture factors at work in any organization, and the results should stimulate brainstorming about how to get them working together even more harmoniously. The Summary Worksheets at the ends of the chapters will become handy documents, providing snapshots of where you have been and where you might head in the future.

Once you have thoroughly assessed each strategy and culture factor, you will finally reassemble them in Chapter 7, where you will create an overall Summary Worksheet and learn how to use the Strategy-Culture Matching Grid. By the end of Chapter 7, you will have determined:

- The current state of your organization's strategy and culture alloy. The execupreneur forges a durable alloy with the six components of strategy and culture, always balancing the need for new strategic directions with the cultural traits of an organization's people.
- Both the strong and weak points in the current alloy. An execupreneur thinks deeply about even the seemingly inconsequential weaknesses in the

organization because today's small problem can grow into tomorrow's crisis.
- Matches and mismatches among the strategy-culture factors. Before embarking on a program of change, an execupreneur looks into every nook and cranny of the organization's strategy and culture.
- How adjustments in any one factor might affect the others. In a dynamic organization an execupreneur constantly weighs the subtle ways in which a change in one factor can affect all the other factors.

We should caution you to be patient as you complete the assessment portion of the workbook. Although you've embarked on an evaluation of your organization with the ultimate goal of better positioning yourself to anticipate and take advantage of change, before you take action you must figure out where you've been and where you are now. The Future Directions section at the end of each summary worksheet will let you do a little brainstorming about possible future action, but bear in mind that hasty action after too little assessment can lead to harmful adjustments and block your path toward excellence.

But once you have finished the first seven chapters, created an overall Summary Worksheet, and learned how to use the Strategy-Culture Matching Grid, you will be ready to take action in Part II, where you will have an opportunity to apply all that you have learned to four classic cases. Regardless of your own organization's present status, you should be able to relate to at least one of these four kinds of companies:

1. Type D organizations with poor strategies and poor cultures
2. Type C organizations with rich strategies but poor cultures
3. Type B organizations with rich cultures but poor strategies
4. Type A organizations striving to maintain rich cultures and rich strategies

Each of these situations demands it own special action. Obviously, a Type D organization is in deep trouble and may require sweeping alterations in every aspect of its business. Since our experience has taught us that you can modify your strategies much more easily than the culture you have taken so long to build, Type C organizations pose the second most difficult challenge, while Type B organizations pose the third. Even if you enjoy a durable alloy, a Type A organization, you will have to work diligently to protect its strength as your business environment continues to change at an accelerated pace.

We think this book is unique in the way it tries to translate ideas about management into a genuine program for improvement. You could hire a consultant to do all this for you, but no outsider knows your company, your customers, and your competitors as well as you do, and no consultant knows or cares as deeply about your people, their commitment, competence, and consistency. With this workbook as a sort of "facilitator," you can now take the first steps toward becoming an execupreneur.

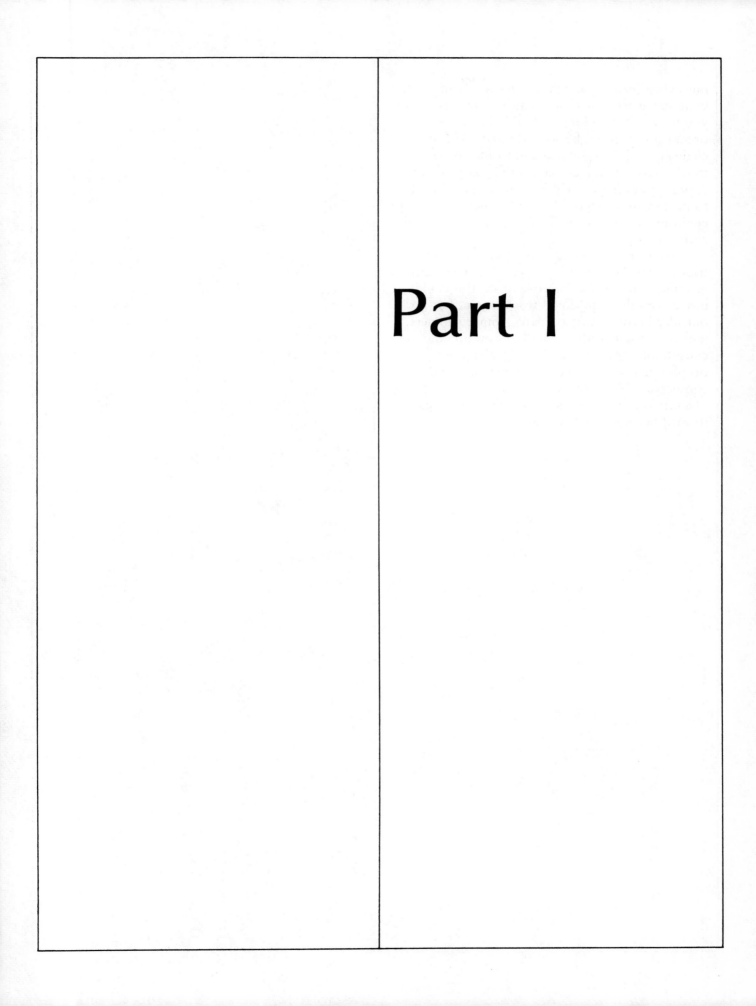

Part I

CHAPTER 1

SATISFYING CUSTOMER NEEDS

The "Burger Wars" between McDonald's, Burger King, and Wendy's have grown so intense that in their television commercials the companies have begun to viciously attack one another's perceived weaknesses. When the dust settles, however, the winner will not be the company that developed the cleverest slogan ("Where's the beef?") but the one that best satisfies its customers' appetite for a quick meal.

Not long ago researchers at Burger King's labs calculated that people prefer hamburgers at precisely 130 degrees. Could the company satisfy this need by positioning a heat lamp over the waiting burgers? That seemed like a simple solution, but the new lamps not only warmed the Whoppers, they heated the drinks as well; and hot cola could send customers scurrying to a competitor up the street. Eventually an enterprising Des Moines Burger King manager solved the problem by inventing a sheet metal shield that would focus heat on the Whopper bin but deflect it from the drinks. As a result, customers at Burger King throughout the world can now enjoy uniformly hot Whoppers and ice-cold drinks. Clearly, this is the sort of tactic that wins battles in the "Burger Wars."

Successful strategies depend on attention to even the most minor customer needs. No matter what kind of customers you serve, whether industrial or consumer, eager or suspicious, unless your product or service genuinely meets their needs, you won't stay in business long. Regardless of the products or services you offer, you are really selling satisfaction of needs or solutions to problems; as Charles Revson once said, "In the factory we make cosmetics. In the store we sell hope."

Levi Strauss & Company, long heralded as the world's leading blue jeans maker, seemed to possess almost clairvoyant insight into the practical clothing needs of millions of people all over the world. During the 1970s the demand for Levi jeans rose to such heights that retailers could sell every pair of jeans they received from the manufacturer. However, this comfortable position led Levi Strauss to shift its focus away from its customers and markets and inward toward increasing production, building new factories, and securing more raw materials to meet the apparently insatiable demand for its product. Then, in the 1980s, sales of traditional blue jeans slackened as the market moved toward more fashionable jeans, a development that for the first time in its history put Levi Strauss in a catch-up position. Unfortunately, the company had become so internally focused on meeting what it mistakenly assumed to be an unlimited demand that it paid too little attention to the shift in customer preferences. When Levi Strauss could not respond fast enough to this trend, it ended up distancing itself still further from its customers and the retailers to whom the inward focus of the company had made Levi seem aloof and rigid. Levi's unwillingness to participate in co-op advertising or support store promotions had offended retailers so much that the declining demand for blue jeans left Levi without the loyal distributors it needed to introduce more competitive products. After a three-year earnings slide beginning in 1980 and arrested only briefly in 1983, Levi Strauss earnings dropped 79 percent in 1984, from $195 million to $41 million.

For a sharply contrasting example, take a look at the fast-moving Thompson Medical Company, a dietary aids manufacturer that has displayed remarkable sensitivity to its customers' desires. Thompson Medical produces the nonprescription Dexatrim, an appetite suppressant in capsule form, and Slim-Fast, a meal replacement mix that dieters combine with skim milk. Just as there always seems to be a new diet book on the best-seller lists, there always seems to be a new diet fad to which millions of Americans will flock. First, dieters wanted appetite suppressants; then, as controversy began to surround the safety of such products, they switched their allegiance to meal replacements. Each time Thompson rode to the rescue, first with Dexatrim and now with Slim-Fast. Every week the company receives hundreds of letters from satisfied customers. When the market shifts again, Thompson promises to be there. The company's overriding goal of helping people who can't muster the willpower or don't have the natural metabolism to stay thin has helped Thompson fatten its own bottom line in the last five years from earnings of $4.7 million on sales of $50 million to earnings of $23 million on sales of $215 million. Today, Thompson dominates both the appetite-suppressant and meal-replacement market segments with 60 to 70 percent market shares.

To satisfy your own customers' needs you must take three crucial steps:

Step A: *Locate customer segments*
Step B: *Assess customer needs*
Step C: *Anticipate changes in segments and needs*

Since a company's customer segments and the needs of those segments constantly fluctuate in our fast-changing world, you must use new and creative methods for locating your segments. Only then can you anticipate further changes, thereby inventing rather than merely suffering through the future.

STEP A
LOCATE CUSTOMER SEGMENTS

First, you must identify and understand every different and distinct customer segment in your markets. To do so we suggest that you separately analyze each of your product lines or service groupings to ensure specific and focused understanding of the segments they serve. Since you can never assume that understanding of one segment will automatically enable you to understand another, always look for even the most seemingly insignificant differences among segments.

In the words of Theodore Levitt, the renowned marketing professor at the Harvard Business School, "If you're not thinking segments, you're not thinking." To effectively "think segments" you must carefully consider the differences among your customers. What drives different groups to make different choices? What causes different groups to perceive and value your product or service differently? Don't settle for the obvious answers. Although most executives grasp the usual demographic, buying-habit, and product-use distinctions between customer groups, few plunge below the surface for the deeper understanding that allows anticipation and unprecedented satisfaction of needs.

EXERCISE 1
CREATIVELY SEGMENTING CUSTOMERS

What methods of segmentation do you currently favor? Do you usually define your customers on the basis of their income, geographical location, use of your product, or point of purchase? If not, you should now. Begin Exercise 1 with these four methods of segmentation, then identify *additional* methods of segmentation, such as customer objectives, customer expectations, information or service requirements, decision-making process, or perceived value. Any new way of perceiving your customers should help you do a better job of predicting and satisfying their needs.

A new segmentation method tremendously benefited a $70 million sign-making company and its customers. We will refer to it as Landon Corporation. Landon produced all kinds of electric, painted, engraved, individualized-letter, exterior, and interior signs. You name it, Landon made it. For twenty years the company had enjoyed an enviable reputation as a quality sign maker in the Northwest. Recently, however, it had suffered at the hands of intensified regional and national competition. Sales had stagnated at the $70 million mark for the past two years, and Phil Landon, son of the company's founder, knew he was losing market share. To remedy the situation, he sought advice from a few close friends who ran similar operations in other parts of the country. One of these friends suggested that Phil reorient the way he viewed his customers. "Instead of dealing with customers according to the *kind* of sign they want," the friend advised Phil, "start dealing with them according to the *purposes* they expect their sign to fulfill." For several weeks Phil did so, segmenting his customers not by kind (electronic, painted, metal letter, interior, or exterior) but by purpose (to give instructions, to create an image, to identify a location, or to sell a product). When he applied this new method of segmentation to a number of recent sales, he discovered that some of his most valuable customers had purchased the wrong kind of sign for a given purpose. The exercise revealed to Phil that his company had been much too willing to accept the customer's determination of the type of sign needed to get the job done. But isn't the customer always right? Not always.

As Phil dug deeper into this new method of segmenting his customers, he discovered that in fact some of his customers had gone to competitors because Landon was not taking the time to help them tailor products to their purposes. Before long, Phil used the insight gained through the new method of segmenting customers to completely revamp Landon's marketing approach to make sure Landon sales-people determined a "sign's purpose" before taking an order. This simple adjustment in the way Landon viewed its customers forced the company's sales staff to become deeply involved with customer needs, and it got immediate results. In the year following the new segmentation method Landon's sales increased a full 20 percent, to just under $85 million. And, most important, Landon's customers expressed greater satisfaction than ever, because they were not only getting quality signs, but were also getting the right sign for the right purpose. Below is an example of how Phil completed one portion of Exercise 1.

EXERCISE 1 EXAMPLE

1. **Segmentation Method:** *Sign's Purpose*

   Rank in Terms of Insight, Benefit:

   A. **Insights Gained:** *Customers seldom fully understand or analyze a proposed sign's purpose, thus their real needs go unmet.*

   B. **Does this method help you better satisfy customer needs? Why? How?** *Yes, because customers ultimately want signs that meet their real needs. With this method of segmentation we can do a better job of making sure customers get the right kinds of signs for their purposes.*

A few cautions before you put your own customers through Exercise 1. If you do not routinely use the "customer objectives"

segmentation method, be sure to include it as one of your new methods. When you use customer objectives as a means of segmentation, consider *all* possible objectives that customers may have when buying your product. Their different objectives become different segments. Plan to spend a minimum of two concentrated hours just thinking about additional methods of segmentation, having gathered and studied appropriate market research data beforehand. Intel recently adopted a different customer segmentation method, looking specifically at "customer thinking processes and attitudes." With this new way of looking at customer segments, Intel found that some segments were worried about the speed and power of microchips while others were more worried about software. The new distinction helped the company redirect its educational and marketing efforts. Perform this exercise separately for each of your company's businesses or product/service groups.

EXERCISE 1 WORKSHEET

Creatively Segmenting Customers

1. Segmentation Method: _____
   _____

   Rank in Terms
   of Insight, Benefit: ☐

   A. Insights Gained: _____
      _____
      _____
      _____
      _____
      _____

   B. Does this method help you better
      satisfy customer needs? Why? How?
      _____
      _____
      _____
      _____
      _____
      _____

2. Segmentation Method: _____
   _____

   Rank in Terms
   of Insight, Benefit: ☐

   A. Insights Gained: _____
      _____
      _____
      _____
      _____

   B. Does this method help you better
      satisfy customer needs? Why? How?
      _____
      _____

_____
_____
_____
_____

3. Segmentation Method: _____
   _____

   Rank in Terms
   of Insight, Benefit: ☐

   A. Insights Gained: _____
      _____
      _____
      _____
      _____
      _____

   B. Does this method help you better
      satisfy customer needs? Why? How?
      _____
      _____
      _____
      _____
      _____

4. Segmentation Method: _____
   _____

   Rank in Terms
   of Insight, Benefit: ☐

   A. Insights Gained: _____
      _____
      _____
      _____
      _____

   B. Does this method help you better
      satisfy customer needs? Why? How?
      _____
      _____

EXERCISE 1 WORKSHEET (*Cont.*)

_____
_____
_____
_____
_____

5. Segmentation Method: _____

Rank in Terms
of Insight, Benefit: ☐

A. Insights Gained: _____
   _____
   _____
   _____
   _____
   _____

B. Does this method help you better
   satisfy customer needs? Why? How?
   _____
   _____
   _____
   _____
   _____
   _____

6. Segmentation Method: _____

Rank in Terms
of Insight, Benefit: ☐

A. Insights Gained: _____
   _____
   _____
   _____
   _____

B. Does this method help you better
   satisfy customer needs? Why? How?
   _____
   _____
   _____
   _____
   _____
   _____

7. Segmentation Method: _____

Rank in Terms
of Insight, Benefit: ☐

A. Insights Gained: _____
   _____
   _____
   _____
   _____
   _____

B. Does this method help you better
   satisfy customer needs? Why? How?
   _____
   _____
   _____
   _____
   _____

EXERCISE 2
TARGETING CUSTOMER SEGMENTS

This exercise will help you better understand how different customer segments relate to your company's products or services. To return to our example of Landon Corporation, Phil discovered many previously ignored customer segments when he began using the "sign's purpose" segmentation method. Although one of these segments wanted to accomplish multiple purposes with one sign, experience had taught Phil that no sign can do "all things for all people." One customer, a men's suit manufacturer, operated a factory in an out-of-the-way spot and needed a sign near the freeway to give directions. In addition to directions the manufacturer wanted to communicate through this same sign that the factory was the largest textile facility in the region, that the company's regional sales office was also housed at the same location, that the facility was open to retailers every day from 9 A.M. to 4 P.M., and that the factory held semiannual clearance sales that were open to the public.

Phil could never make such customers happy because the resultant signs ended up doing "nothing for anyone." Therefore, he determined to help "multiple objective" customers identify the *major* purpose of the sign and let that purpose dictate the nature of the sign. He relabeled this customer segment "uneducated buyers." Phil filled out a section of Exercise 2 in the following way.

EXERCISE 2 EXAMPLE

1. **Customer Segment:** *Uneducated Buyers*
   A. **Customer Segment Characteristics:**

% of Whole Market	35%
% of Company Sales in Segment	45%
% of Market Share in Segment	50%
Projected % of Growth in 1–5 Years	15%

   B. **Current Level of Customer Satisfaction:**
   ☐ High
   ☐ Medium
   ☒ Low

   C. **Opportunities for Improving Market Share:** *Opportunities are great since no other competitors are trying to resolve this segment's needs.*

The new method also allowed Phil to break down another segment, "instructional buyers," into three subsegments: those who need signs telling directions, what you will find inside, and the best way to do something. The men's suit manufacturer was really an instructional buyer once Phil educated the company regarding the purpose of signs. Together with Phil the customer decided that the primary purpose of the sign should be to instruct freeway drivers on how to find the factory and offices. The benefit of this new method of segmentation was already paying off for Phil, and his continuing evaluation uncovered many other previously unrecognized segments.

Using your preferred former segmentation method and the most promising *new* method, critically evaluate your own customer segments. Whether your company has only a few or many businesses or product/service groups, put each business or product/service group through Exercise 2. If your company has several businesses or product/service groups you might want to photocopy Exercise 2 in order to have sufficient space to evaluate the segments associated with each business or product/service group.

EXERCISE 2 WORKSHEET

Targeting Customer Segments

1. Customer Segment: _____

   A. **Customer Segment Characteristics:**
      % of Whole Market _____
      % of Company Sales in Segment _____
      % of Market Share in Segment _____
      Projected % of Growth
      in 1−5 Years
      _____

   B. **Current Level of**   ☐ High
      Customer Satisfaction: ☐ Medium
                                      ☐ Low

   C. **Opportunities for Improving**
      Market Share: _____
      _____
      _____
      _____
      _____
      _____
      _____
      _____

2. Customer Segment: _____

   A. **Customer Segment Characteristics:**
      % of Whole Market _____
      % of Company Sales in Segment _____
      % of Market Share in Segment _____
      Projected % of Growth
      in 1−5 Years
      _____

   B. **Current Level of**   ☐ High
      Customer Satisfaction: ☐ Medium
                                      ☐ Low

   C. **Opportunities for Improving**
      Market Share: _____
      _____
      _____
      _____
      _____
      _____
      _____

3. Customer Segment: _____

   A. **Customer Segment Characteristics:**
      % of Whole Market _____
      % of Company Sales in Segment _____
      % of Market Share in Segment _____
      Projected % of Growth
      in 1−5 Years
      _____

   B. **Current Level of**   ☐ High
      Customer Satisfaction: ☐ Medium
                                      ☐ Low

   C. **Opportunities for Improving**
      Market Share: _____
      _____
      _____
      _____
      _____
      _____
      _____

4. Customer Segment: _____

   A. **Customer Segment Characteristics:**
      % of Whole Market _____
      % of Company Sales in Segment _____
      % of Market Share in Segment _____
      Projected % of Growth
      in 1−5 Years
      _____

   B. **Current Level of**   ☐ High
      Customer Satisfaction: ☐ Medium
                                      ☐ Low

   C. **Opportunities for Improving**
      Market Share: _____
      _____
      _____
      _____
      _____
      _____
      _____

5. Customer Segment: _____

   A. Customer Segment Characteristics:
      % of Whole Market _____
      % of Company Sales in Segment _____
      % of Market Share in Segment _____
      Projected % of Growth
      in 1–5 Years

      _____

   B. Current Level of   ☐ High
      Customer Satisfaction: ☐ Medium
                            ☐ Low

   C. Opportunities for Improving
      Market Share: _____

      _____
      _____
      _____
      _____
      _____
      _____

6. Customer Segment: _____

   A. Customer Segment Characteristics:
      % of Whole Market _____
      % of Company Sales in Segment _____
      % of Market Share in Segment _____
      Projected % of Growth
      in 1–5 Years

      _____

   B. Current Level of   ☐ High
      Customer Satisfaction: ☐ Medium
                            ☐ Low

   C. Opportunities for Improving
      Market Share: _____

      _____
      _____
      _____
      _____
      _____
      _____

7. Customer Segment: _____

   A. Customer Segment Characteristics:
      % of Whole Market _____
      % of Company Sales in Segment _____
      % of Market Share in Segment _____
      Projected % of Growth
      in 1–5 Years

      _____

   B. Current Level of   ☐ High
      Customer Satisfaction: ☐ Medium
                            ☐ Low

   C. Opportunities for Improving
      Market Share: _____

      _____
      _____
      _____
      _____
      _____
      _____

8. Customer Segment: _____

   A. Customer Segment Characteristics:
      % of Whole Market _____
      % of Company Sales in Segment _____
      % of Market Share in Segment _____
      Projected % of Growth
      in 1–5 Years

      _____

   B. Current Level of   ☐ High
      Customer Satisfaction: ☐ Medium
                            ☐ Low

   C. Opportunities for Improving
      Market Share: _____

      _____
      _____
      _____
      _____
      _____
      _____

9. Customer Segment: _____

    A. Customer Segment Characteristics:
       % of Whole Market _____
       % of Company Sales in Segment _____
       % of Market Share in Segment _____
       Projected % of Growth
       in 1–5 Years

      _____

    B. Current Level of   ☐ High
       Customer Satisfaction: ☐ Medium
                         ☐ Low

    C. Opportunities for Improving
       Market Share: _____
      _____
      _____
      _____
      _____
      _____
      _____

10. Customer Segment: _____

    A. Customer Segment Characteristics:
       % of Whole Market _____
       % of Company Sales in Segment _____
       % of Market Share in Segment _____
       Projected % of Growth
       in 1–5 Years

      _____

    B. Current Level of   ☐ High
       Customer Satisfaction: ☐ Medium
                         ☐ Low

    C. Opportunities for Improving
       Market Share: _____
      _____
      _____
      _____
      _____
      _____
      _____

STEP B

ASSESS CUSTOMER NEEDS

Once you have located segments, you can consider the needs of each segment in detail. By "needs" we mean anything a customer wants, requires, or demands. It can be a basic human need such as food, clothing, or shelter, or it can be an impulsive desire such as an urge to own a Cabbage Patch doll. Whether you are trying to meet an existing customer need or are hoping to create a new one, the basic requirement remains the same: you must genuinely satisfy the need.

It may seem obvious that you should always attempt to find out what your customers want, require, or demand and then do everything possible to satisfy those needs, but you must always weigh whether you can do so profitably. By the same token, although you should seldom take any action that would produce less than an adequate return, you should contemplate the consequences of *failing* to meet a given need. If a need is critical to attracting and keeping customers, you may have to redirect your efforts toward more reachable customer segments, or you may have to devise creative ways to enhance your financial return. All this assumes that you have forged a strong strategy-culture alloy in the first place. However, if deficiencies exist, you may need to make certain adjustments before you attempt to satisfy an important customer need. We will consider such situations in Part II of this book, but for now Exercises 3 and 4 will help you increase your understanding of the specific needs of the customer segments pinpointed in Exercises 1 and 2.

EXERCISE 3
IDENTIFYING THE NEEDS OF EACH SEGMENT

When you consider the major desires, requirements, and demands of each of your customer segments, do not limit yourself to your own company's products or services, but consider the broad range of products or services offered by competitors in your industry. To accurately identify customer needs you must become extremely specific. Otherwise you might not address all the relevant differences among segments. To help ensure that you do so, Exercise 3 requires that you identify needs related to product marketing characteristics. These include facts about the attributes of a product or service most desired by the customer segment, its sensitivity to price, its need for information about the product or service, its demands for reassurance of performance, its expectations regarding sales and service, the effects of advertising and promotion on decisions to buy, and other marketing considerations, such as after-sale service. When Phil Landon went through the process of identifying the needs of his uneducated buyers" segment he gained some interesting insights:

EXERCISE 3 EXAMPLE

Customer Needs Relative to:	Company's Ability to Meet Needs:
A. **Product or Service Attributes**	S = Superior
B. **Price of Product or Service**	G = Good
	F = Fair
C. **Information About Product or Service**	P = Poor
D. **Reassurance of Performance**	
E. **Sales and Distribution of Product or Service**	
F. **Advertising and Promotion of Product or Service**	
G. **Other**	

Customer Segment: *Uneducated Buyers*

A. *Customers in this segment wrongly expect one sign to serve several different purposes.*   P

B. *The price of the sign does not matter as much as results.*   P

C. *This segment needs to be more carefully informed about what signs can and cannot achieve, but they seldom realize that they need more information until after they receive it.*   F

D. *Customers in this segment want guarantees regarding the ability of the sign to achieve multiple goals, but don't really expect to get those guarantees.*   G

E. *This segment prefers salespeople who project images of knowledgeable experts, who will write clear orders and deliver the sign on time.*   S

F. *Customers in this segment respond to advertising that stresses the sort of all-purpose sign that seldom gets desired results.*   P

G. *Service after the sale becomes extremely important in cases where the sign doesn't work properly or works properly but does not produce expected results.*   S

Although Phil found some major mismatches between customer needs and the way his company delivered its products and services, he also saw the opportunity to educate customers and as a result better serve their real needs, install more signs, and reduce service costs.

You should complete Exercise 3 for all the customer segments you targeted in Exercise 2. Remember, different customers display different needs, even though those differences may be subtle. Paying attention to even the subtlest differences can reap huge rewards in terms of satisfied customers.

With these marketing characteristics in mind, you can begin assessing your company's current effectiveness at satisfying needs.

Identifying the Needs of Each Segment

Customer Needs Relative to:	Company's Ability to Meet Needs:
A. Product or Service Attributes	S = Superior
B. Price of Product or Service	G = Good
C. Information About Product or Service	F = Fair
D. Reassurance of Performance	P = Poor
E. Sales and Distribution of Product or Service	
F. Advertising and Promotion of Product or Service	
G. Other	

Customer Segment: _____

A. _____ ☐
_____
_____

B. _____ ☐
_____
_____

C. _____ ☐
_____
_____

D. _____ ☐
_____
_____

E. _____ ☐
_____
_____

F. _____ ☐
_____
_____

G. _____ ☐
_____
_____

Customer Segment: _____

A. _____ ☐
_____
_____

B. _____ ☐
_____
_____

C. _____ ☐
_____
_____

D. _____ ☐
_____
_____

E. _____ ☐
_____
_____

F. _____ ☐
_____
_____

G. _____ ☐
_____
_____

Customer Segment: _____

A. _____ ☐
_____
_____

B. _____ ☐
_____
_____

C. _____ ☐
_____
_____

EXERCISE 3 WORKSHEET (*Cont.*)

D. _____ ☐
_____
_____

E. _____ ☐
_____
_____

F. _____ ☐
_____
_____

G. _____ ☐
_____
_____

Customer Segment: _____

A. _____ ☐
_____
_____

B. _____ ☐
_____
_____

C. _____ ☐
_____
_____

D. _____ ☐
_____
_____

E. _____ ☐
_____
_____

F. _____ ☐
_____
_____

G. _____ ☐
_____
_____

Customer Segment: _____

A. _____ ☐
_____
_____

B. _____ ☐
_____
_____

C. _____ ☐
_____
_____

D. _____ ☐
_____
_____

E. _____ ☐
_____
_____

F. _____ ☐
_____
_____

G. _____ ☐
_____
_____

EXERCISE 4
MEASURING EACH SEGMENT'S LEVEL OF SATISFACTION

Using the ratings assigned in Exercise 3, complete the chart below by grouping needs according to the degree to which you satisfy them. Such a grouping offers a simple yet comprehensive picture of how your company's products and services rate in terms of satisfying the specific needs of different segments. The following is how Exercise 4 looked for Phil Landon's "uneducated" segment.

EXERCISE 4 EXAMPLE

Customer Segment: *Uneducated Buyers*

Needs That Are Satisfied in a "Superior" Way
1. *Need for knowledgeable salespeople*
2. *Need for service on faulty or unsuccessful signs*

Needs That Are Satisfied in a "Good" Way
1. *Need for guarantees*

Needs That Are Satisfied in a "Fair" Way
1. *Need for information*

Needs That Are Satisfied in a "Poor" Way
1. *Need for one sign to fulfill all purposes*
2. *Need for performance over price*
3. *Need for advertising to choose sign company*

Now you can proceed with your own Exercise 4, the results of which should help you gain a new perspective on your company's performance in meeting the needs of particular segments.

Measuring Each Segment's Level of Satisfaction

Customer Segment: _____

Needs That Are Satisfied in a "Superior" Way

1. _____

2. _____

3. _____

Needs That Are Satisfied in a "Good" Way

1. _____

2. _____

3. _____

Needs That Are Satisfied in a "Fair" Way

1. _____

2. _____

3. _____

Needs That Are Satisfied in a "Poor" Way

1. _____

2. _____

3. _____

Customer Segment: _____

Needs That Are Satisfied in a "Superior" Way

1. _____

2. _____

3. _____

Needs That Are Satisfied in a "Good" Way

1. _____

2. _____

3. _____

Needs That Are Satisfied in a "Fair" Way

1. _____

2. _____

3. _____

Needs That Are Satisfied in a "Poor" Way

1. _____

2. _____

3. _____

Customer Segment: _____

Needs That Are Satisfied in a "Superior" Way

1. _____

2. _____

3. _____

Needs That Are Satisfied in a "Good" Way

1. _____

2. _____

3. _____

Needs That Are Satisfied in a "Fair" Way

1. _____

2. _____

3. _____

Needs That Are Satisfied in a "Poor" Way

    1. _____

_____

    2. _____

_____

    3. _____

_____

Customer Segment: _____

Needs That Are Satisfied in a "Superior" Way

    1. _____

_____

    2. _____

_____

    3. _____

_____

Needs That Are Satisfied in a "Good" Way

    1. _____

_____

    2. _____

_____

    3. _____

_____

Needs That Are Satisfied in a "Fair" Way

    1. _____

_____

    2. _____

_____

    3. _____

_____

Needs That Are Satisfied in a "Poor" Way

    1. _____

_____

    2. _____

_____

    3. _____

_____

Customer Segment: _____

Needs That Are Satisfied in a "Superior" Way

    1. _____

_____

    2. _____

_____

    3. _____

_____

Needs That Are Satisfied in a "Good" Way

    1. _____

_____

    2. _____

_____

    3. _____

_____

Needs That Are Satisfied in a "Fair" Way

    1. _____

_____

    2. _____

_____

    3. _____

_____

Needs That Are Satisfied in a "Poor" Way

    1. _____

_____

    2. _____

_____

    3. _____

_____

STEP C

ANTICIPATE CHANGES IN SEGMENTS AND NEEDS

After you have examined segments and needs, you must thoroughly analyze any changes that might occur or that you might cause to occur. Since customer segments and needs shift as surely and inevitably as the tides—sometimes in small, almost imperceptible ripples, sometimes in massive waves—you can never count on filling the needs of a particular customer segment indefinitely but must remain ever poised to respond to or initiate change.

No company can remain excellent unless it effectively responds to and even invents change. As customer segments and needs continually evolve, you must remain ever alert for the early and often subtle occurrences that signal an impending change. Changes come in all sizes: major ones that strike quickly, such as the deregulation of the airline industry; major ones that take time to develop, such as the growth of the fast-food industry; and minor ones, such as the invention of Velcro, that can offer a major opportunity to an aggressive entrepreneur. By paying close attention to changes, you can seize opportunities that will leave your competitors shaking their heads and muttering "Why didn't *I* think of that?"

EXERCISE 5
DETERMINING CHANGES IN CUSTOMER SEGMENTS

This exercise should enable you to anticipate any changes in the nature of the customer segments identified in the previous exercises. Continue to use your two preferred methods for segmenting customers. For each customer segment you will be looking for any and all changes, regardless of the extent to which you now think they might affect your business. Pay special attention to the cause of the change, whether it will most likely increase or decrease, and what the change might mean to your industry as a whole. Build and test your scenarios thoroughly, forecasting both better-than-expected and worse-than-expected results. As Phil Landon reviewed how his segments might be changing, he determined that the "image sign" segment was growing rapidly and would most likely continue to expand for the next five years. Image signs are those that create desired images in the minds of prospective customers. For example, one of Phil's customers was a Las Vegas casino that had recently refurbished its hotel and casino and wanted to create a new "bigger and better" image. Landon Corporation was engaged to create an image of "new life" for this casino by constructing one of the largest electronic signs in Las Vegas. Had Phil not carefully considered the changing nature of the image-sign segment, he might have missed an important opportunity. Phil completed Exercise 5 in the following manner.

EXERCISE 5 EXAMPLE

A. **Anticipated Change(s)**
B. **Cause of Change(s)**
C. **Are Changes Increasing or Decreasing?**
D. **Implications for Your Company**

Customer Segment: *Image Signs*

A. *Higher growth in this segment over next five years.*

B. *Greater awareness on the part of customers regarding the value of image signs.*
C. *Changes are increasing rapidly.*
D. *We need to beef up our understanding of image signs so we are prepared to deal knowledgeably with customers' needs in this segment.*

Determining Changes in Customer Segments

A. Anticipated Change(s)
B. Cause of Change(s)
C. Are Changes Increasing or Decreasing?
D. Implications for Your Company

Customer Segment: _____

    A. _____

_____

    B. _____

_____

    C. _____

_____

    D. _____

_____

Customer Segment: _____

    A. _____

_____

    B. _____

_____

    C. _____

_____

    D. _____

_____

Customer Segment: _____

    A. _____

_____

    B. _____

_____

    C. _____

_____

    D. _____

_____

Customer Segment: _____

    A. _____

_____

    B. _____

_____

    C. _____

_____

    D. _____

_____

Customer Segment: _____

    A. _____

_____

    B. _____

_____

    C. _____

_____

    D. _____

_____

EXERCISE 6
ISOLATING CHANGES IN CUSTOMER NEEDS

Just as you did for Exercise 5, complete the Exercise 6 Worksheet, focusing on any customer need you expect to change. The American automobile industry, unable to see customer needs changing, believed America would drive whatever Detroit produced. That mistake opened the floodgates to small, economical imported cars. And remember Levi Strauss, who thought they could keep cranking out good old blue jeans forever?

Phil Landon benefited from this exercise by determining that the needs of customers in several segments were gravitating toward more information about what signs can and cannot be expected to do. This was good news because it drew on one of his company's perennial strengths, even though in the past Landon had not done a very good job of marketing this expertise.

Isolating Changes
in Customer Needs

A. Anticipated Change(s)
B. Cause of the Change(s)
C. Are Changes Increasing or Decreasing?
D. Implications for Your Company

Customer Segment: _____

    A. _____

    B. _____

    C. _____

    D. _____

Customer Segment: _____

    A. _____

    B. _____

    C. _____

    D. _____

Customer Segment: _____

    A. _____

    B. _____

    C. _____

    D. _____

Customer Segment: _____

    A. _____

    B. _____

    C. _____

    D. _____

Customer Segment: _____

    A. _____

    B. _____

    C. _____

    D. _____

SUMMARY

Now you can reduce the information and insights from these six exercises into a summary worksheet, writing three to six *overall* conclusions about your company's methods of satisfying customer needs. Fewer than three indicate too little thinking, more than six too little synthesizing. If you have completed more than one set of exercises for different businesses or product/service groupings, you should pull it all together into one summary of conclusions. The following is a sampling from Phil Landon's conclusions.

SUMMARY EXAMPLE

PART A

Conclusions from Step A, Exercises 1 and 2

The customer segment that looks most promising in terms of size is the segment that does not fully understand the importance of isolating the major purpose of a planned sign.

PART B

Conclusions from Step B, Exercises 3 and 4

Our products and services will not meet the needs of the "uneducated buyer" unless we add an educational component into marketing efforts.

PART C

Conclusions from Step C, Exercises 5 and 6

An educational campaign will coincide perfectly with the increasing need for more information.

PART D

Overall Summary of Conclusions

All of our targeted customer segments will respond to greater expertise on our part and to more thorough information before buying.

PART E

Future Directions

Write and publish an illustrated booklet with humorous and interesting historical examples of the ways signs can be used to accomplish certain purposes. This could be an entertaining way to educate our customers.

Spend some time brainstorming ideas for the last section of the summary worksheet, Future Directions. This section should contain the insights and ideas that can move you beyond the assessment stage to the action stage. In what specific ways can you improve or enhance your company's ability to satisfy customer needs? When Phil Landon did some brainstorming, he hit upon the idea of a brochure on the purposes of signs.

SUMMARY WORKSHEET

PART A

Conclusions from Step A, Exercises 1 and 2, pages 7–12

1. _____

2. _____

3. _____

PART B

Conclusions from Step B, Exercises 3 and 4, pages 15–19

1. _____

2. _____

3. _____

PART C

Conclusions from Step C, Exercises 5 and 6, pages 22–24

1. _____

2. _____

3. _____

PART D

Overall Summary of Conclusions

1. _____

2. _____

3. _____

4. _____

5. _____
_____
_____
_____
_____
_____

6. _____
_____
_____
_____
_____

PART E

Future Directions

_____
_____
_____
_____
_____
_____
_____
_____
_____
_____
_____
_____
_____

If employees are the heart of a company, then customers are its lifeblood. One moment's inattention to the well-being of your customers and the satisfaction of their ever-changing needs can rob your organization of its excellence. One slip, one miscalculation, one smug assumption can allow your competitors to woo them away. In the next chapter you will learn to analyze the impact of your competitors on your ongoing struggle to satisfy customer needs.

CHAPTER 2

SUSTAINING COMPETITIVE ADVANTAGE

Ever since Federal Express burst onto the scene, the overnight mail service industry has been growing like wildfire. Overnight service satisfies such a vital need that it will continue to grow, and more and more competitors will jump into the fray. Given this environment, the industry offers an interesting illustration of the importance of sustaining competitive advantage.

While pioneering Federal Express continues to dominate the field and to provide a model for the industry, its competitors continually force the company to work around the clock to maintain its position. UPS recently entered the market, hoping to gain a unique advantage by combining its successful large-package service with overnight delivery, and the U.S. Postal Service has introduced late-night drop-offs to enhance its relatively lower-priced Express Mail service. Then Emery Air Freight rebounded with its focus on big-package shipments, DHL with a vigorous attack on the international market, and Airborne with a decision to butt heads and try to "out-Federal" Federal.

Pressured from all sides, Federal has begun discounting certain services and has introduced ZapMail, electronically whisking documents anywhere in the U.S. in less than two hours. Rival Purolator, concluding that development of its own electronic mail route was too risky, has agreed to deliver MCI Mail, a system that MCI Communications Corporation believes can make ZapMail eventually obsolete by using the personal computer. In an industry where keeping track of the competitors is like watching a multisided chess match where every player's move affects the subsequent moves of the other players, every innovative idea deserves quick but careful consideration. Even the slightest miscalculation of an opponent's strategy can spell doom.

Because successful strategies always depend on creating a sustainable competitive advantage, every business faces a similar challenge. No matter what your field, whether intensely competitive and growing or lethargic and declining, unless you can find a way to gain and maintain advantages over your competitors you'll never achieve the sort of long-term success that leads to corporate excellence.

What happens when you pay too little attention to competitive advantage? A decade ago Hattori Seiko Company entered the world watch market, immediately exploiting the weaknesses of the formerly dominant Swiss companies, such as Longine, whose strategy had long been committed to producing fine watches based on painstaking attention to all aspects of a watch's design. This drive to exploit Longine's weaknesses—tradition-bound external design, high production costs, and slow response to changes in fashion—helped Seiko achieve superior external design, lower-cost production techniques, and a prompt response to consumer fads and trends. First targeting the middle-priced watch market with the "instrument look" (digitals, chronographs, miniature calculators, and the like), Seiko then moved to the lower- and higher-priced markets, continuing to build on its three basic advantages. It worked. By the end of the 1970s, Seiko controlled almost half of the U.S. watch market and the Swiss watch industry had nearly collapsed. However, Swiss bankers rushed to the rescue of their industry by providing a massive cash infusion of $500 million and a consolidation of two companies, Asuag and SSIH, a merger that brought together the Longine's brand and almost all Swiss watch manufacturing. The cash helped the new organization install the latest technologies, and the consolidation helped unite and focus resources.

Today, having benefited from a hard-learned lesson in competitive advantage, Asuag and SSIH have launched an aggressive campaign to recapture their former advantage. In 1984 they introduced Swatches, brightly colored plastic watches that addressed customers' demands for both toughness (the watches are waterproof and shockproof) and trendiness, and they plan to offer more style and panache with banana, raspberry, and mint-scented watches and other Swatch accessories. Still, the Swiss have not yet proven they can sustain such an advantage. Asuag-SSIH recently lost $80 million and may experience continuing losses; and while Swiss bankers have strongly supported their watch industry, their support cannot continue without eventual bottom-line results. And of course, no amount of Swiss recovery will force Seiko to sit idly on the sidelines.

In the financial printing industry, Merrill Corporation has gained advantage at the expense of Bowne & Company. Financial printing involves highly sensitive financial documents such as proxy materials, prospectuses, and other reports that clients often need overnight. Bowne & Company had historically satisfied the financial printing needs of the nation's largest corporations, counting more Fortune 500 companies among its clients than any competitor. However, printing technology has changed dramatically in recent years, and Bowne has not been able to adopt new technologies because of opposition from its union work force. Although Bowne's sales force can sell the company's historical dominance, that alone has not been able to convince customers to remain loyal. By contrast, Merrill Corporation's nonunion, high-tech operation, with a flair for snatching key marketing reps from the competition, has been booming. Merrill's typesetting network utilizes sophisticated equipment, such as transmission lines that link the company's seven branches to a computerized printing facility in St. Paul. In order to tap the network of long-standing relationships among investment bankers, attorneys, accountants, and company executives, Merrill's new branch offices raid the ranks of competitors' marketing reps. As a result Merrill has, in a relatively short time, received business in New York from such companies as Merrill Lynch and Dean Witter. The company's 1984 sales doubled to approximately $24 million, and

it wins high marks for creating competitive advantage in an old, established business long resistant to change.

To sustain competitive advantage you must address three fundamental factors:

Step A: *Assess differences among competitors*
Step B: *Weigh advantage over competitors*
Step C: *Look for sustainability of advantages*

The competitive arena constantly changes as new competitors enter the market and old competitors adopt new tactics. Your success at winning a competitive advantage, then sustaining it over the long term, will depend on how thoroughly and creatively you assess your competitors.

STEP A

ASSESS DIFFERENCES AMONG COMPETITORS

First, you must identify all the differences between your company and your competitors' companies and between your products or services and their products or services. A thorough analysis begins with a close examination of every major activity and function in your company and its rivals. What differences exist between your company's "business stages" and those of your competitors? By business stages we mean the distinct steps a company takes to bring a product or service to the marketplace. These stages may differ from industry to industry, but they generally include research and development, production, distribution, marketing, and sales and service.

After listing the stages, identify the critical support functions that enable a product or service to flow smoothly through them. Support functions may not play obvious roles in the business stages but are nevertheless critical to the delivery of a product or service to the marketplace. They might include such areas as finance and accounting management, human resource management, and legal management.

Just as "thinking segments" helps you better satisfy customer needs, "thinking differences" helps you sustain a competitive advantage. The fewer the differences among competitors, the fewer the opportunities for competitive advantage, unless one of the competitors discovers or creates a *new* difference. To uncover differences you must continually compare and contrast activities at all stages and in all functions. Differences can stem from internal conditions, such as the competence of your marketing people, or from external conditions, such as the reliability of suppliers or the effectiveness of independent distributors. Some executives make the mistake of stopping their quest for differences when they determine the most obvious ones, but the smart strategist applies critical thinking to even the smallest differences.

EXERCISE 1
DEFINING DIFFERENCES AT EACH BUSINESS STAGE AND SUPPORT FUNCTION

By the end of this exercise you should be able to identify all the differences between your company and your competitors. First, you must define your firm's business stages. You might start with R&D or the receiving and inventorying of materials, then go to operations or production, followed by distribution or marketing, and finally sales and service. Remember, whatever your business stages, they provide the clues to exploitable differences. For a service-oriented business these stages may differ a great deal, possibly beginning with idea or program development, then moving to marketing and sales training, through customer presentations and sales to program operations or service delivery, and ending with ongoing customer contact.

List your three major competitors on the chart, lumping all other competitors into a fourth group. If you compete against only two major rivals or more than four, reduce or expand the chart appropriately. For each major competitor and for the one group of minor competitors, describe all the differences at each business stage (Part A) and for each support function (Part B).

For example, a national discount-store chain used this method when competition in a Midwestern city grew alarmingly intense. In this particular city the chain had always dominated the market with its four stores, but recently two new competitors had come to town and were planning to expand. Almost overnight the number of formidable competitors had risen from one to three. A management task force for the national chain, consisting of the four store managers and the regional vice president for the area, began its search for sustainable advantage by labeling the business stages its company followed to get merchandise to its customers:

(A) Property acquisition and store construction
(B) Buying
(C) Store layout and management
(D) Merchandising
(E) Customer service

The task force also identified the company's major support functions:

(A) Inventory control
(B) Finance and accounting
(C) Personnel

Finally the task force began looking for differences between its chain and the new competitors. With respect to one of these new competitors, the task force found that in terms of property acquisition and store construction the competitor had situated two stores in newly developed "strip malls" (small shopping areas with at least one grocery store, a discount or variety store, and a number of smaller shops), whereas the national chain's stores were located in older parts of the city, usually next to a grocery store, but without a lot of neighboring shops.

With respect to buying, this new competitor carried brand-name merchandise at a discount and therefore had designed buying practices that emphasized the sort of brand-name products that enjoyed heavy television advertising and which it could purchase at a hefty discount. On the other hand, the national chain carried significantly fewer brand-name products and adhered to a policy of developing close relationships with product manufacturers who would place the national chain's label on their goods.

In terms of store layout and management, the competitor split its store space into thirds: one third for traditional discount-store items (ranging from clothing to cosmetics), another third for showroom products (higher-priced merchandise such as electrical appliances and cameras, displayed on the floor but obtained by customers from the warehouse), and the last third for the necessary storage of showroom items. By contrast, the national chain displayed and sold every product it offered in one area 50 percent larger than the competitor's.

The two competitors also took different approaches to merchandising. While the new competitor rarely promoted individual products or groups of products but simply advertised its "full selection" of brand-name products at discount prices, the national chain relied heavily on the promotion of individual items, constantly announcing sales and special promotions to attract customers.

And finally, the new competitor did not have a credit-card financing program, but tried to make charge accounts easily available to preferred customers. By contrast, the national chain had its own credit-card program that included 25 million customers nationwide and almost 1 million customers in the local metropolitan area.

When the task force looked at the three support functions, it found that the competitor relied on a computerized inventory control system that streamlined pricing and buying, while the national chain still used an outdated semi-automated system. However, the team found no significant differences in the areas of finance and accounting or personnel.

Part A: Stages

Competitor:	Are Differences Major/Minor?	Differences by Stage:
#1 New Competitor		
A. Property Acquisition and Store Construction	*Major*	A. *Located in strip malls vs. our city center locations*
B. Buying	*Minor*	B. *Brand-name merchandise vs. our private label*
C. Store Layout and Management	*Minor*	C. *Showroom and warehouse space vs. our typical retailing space*
D. Merchandising	*Minor*	D. *Generic advertising and promotion of brand-name merchandise at discount vs. our specific advertising and promotion of individual items*
E. Customer Service	*Major*	E. *No credit-card financing vs. our national credit-card program*

Part B: Functions:

	Are Differences Major/Minor?	Differences by Function:
A. Inventory Control	*Minor*	A. *Computerized inventory control system vs. our somewhat outdated system*
B. Finance and Accounting	*Minor*	B. *No apparent differences*
C. Personnel	*Minor*	C. *No apparent differences*

Bear in mind that by this point the executives had only scratched the surface. They went further in their search for differences, eventually discovering a total of twenty major and twenty-eight minor differences before they felt satisfied that they had finished the exercise. You'll want to be just as thorough in your own consideration.

EXERCISE 1 WORKSHEET

PART A: DEFINING DIFFERENCES AT EACH BUSINESS STAGE

Competitor:	Are Differences Major/Minor?	Differences by Stage:
#1 _____		
Stages		
A. _____	_____	A. _____
_____		
_____		
_____		
B. _____	_____	B. _____
_____		
_____		
_____		
C. _____	_____	C. _____
_____		
_____		
_____		
D. _____	_____	D. _____
_____		
_____		
_____		
E. _____	_____	E. _____
_____		
_____		
_____		
F. _____	_____	F. _____
_____		
_____		
_____		
G. _____	_____	G. _____
_____		
_____		
_____		
H. _____	_____	H. _____
_____		
_____		
_____		

Competitor:

#2 _____

Stages

**Are Differences
Major/Minor?**

Differences by Stage:

A. _____
_____
_____
_____
_____

_____

A. _____

B. _____
_____
_____
_____
_____

_____

B. _____

C. _____
_____
_____
_____
_____

_____

C. _____

D. _____
_____
_____
_____
_____

_____

D. _____

E. _____
_____
_____
_____
_____

_____

E. _____

F. _____
_____
_____
_____

_____

F. _____

G. _____
_____
_____
_____

_____

G. _____

H. _____
_____
_____
_____

_____

H. _____

PART A: DEFINING DIFFERENCES AT EACH BUSINESS STAGE

Competitor:

Are Differences Major/Minor?

Differences by Stage:

#3 _____

Stages

A. _____
_____
_____
_____

_____

A. _____

B. _____
_____
_____
_____

_____

B. _____

C. _____
_____
_____
_____

_____

C. _____

D. _____
_____
_____
_____

_____

D. _____

E. _____
_____
_____
_____

_____

E. _____

F. _____
_____
_____
_____

_____

F. _____

G. _____
_____
_____
_____

_____

G. _____

H. _____
_____
_____
_____

_____

H. _____

Competitor: **Are Differences**   **Differences by Stage:**
                               Major/Minor?

#4 _____

Stages

A. _____   _____   A. _____
   _____
   _____
   _____
   _____

B. _____   _____   B. _____
   _____
   _____
   _____
   _____

C. _____   _____   C. _____
   _____
   _____
   _____
   _____

D. _____   _____   D. _____
   _____
   _____
   _____
   _____

E. _____   _____   E. _____
   _____
   _____
   _____
   _____

F. _____   _____   F. _____
   _____
   _____
   _____
   _____

G. _____   _____   G. _____
   _____
   _____
   _____
   _____

H. _____   _____   H. _____
   _____
   _____
   _____
   _____

PART A: DEFINING DIFFERENCES AT EACH BUSINESS STAGE

Competitor:

Are Differences Major/Minor?

Differences by Stage:

#1 _____

Stages

A. _____ _____ A. _____
_____
_____
_____

B. _____ _____ B. _____
_____
_____
_____

C. _____ _____ C. _____
_____
_____
_____

D. _____ _____ D. _____
_____
_____
_____

E. _____ _____ E. _____
_____
_____
_____

F. _____ _____ F. _____
_____
_____
_____

G. _____ _____ G. _____
_____
_____
_____

H. _____ _____ H. _____
_____
_____
_____

Competitor: **Are Differences**   **Differences by Function:**
                             Major/Minor?

#2 _____

Functions

A. _____   _____   A. _____
   _____
   _____
   _____
   _____

B. _____   _____   B. _____
   _____
   _____
   _____

C. _____   _____   C. _____
   _____
   _____
   _____
   _____

D. _____   _____   D. _____
   _____
   _____
   _____

E. _____   _____   E. _____
   _____
   _____
   _____
   _____

F. _____   _____   F. _____
   _____
   _____
   _____

G. _____   _____   G. _____
   _____
   _____
   _____
   _____

H. _____   _____   H. _____
   _____
   _____
   _____
   _____

PART A: DEFINING DIFFERENCES AT EACH BUSINESS STAGE

Competitor:

Are Differences
Major/Minor?

Differences by Stage:

#3 _____

Stages

A. _____ _____ A. _____
_____
_____
_____

B. _____ _____ B. _____
_____
_____
_____

C. _____ _____ C. _____
_____
_____
_____

D. _____ _____ D. _____
_____
_____
_____

E. _____ _____ E. _____
_____
_____
_____

F. _____ _____ F. _____
_____
_____
_____

G. _____ _____ G. _____
_____
_____
_____

H. _____ _____ H. _____
_____
_____
_____

Competitor: Are Differences   Differences by Function:
                               Major/Minor?
#4 _____

Functions

A. _____   _____   A. _____
   _____
   _____
   _____
   _____

B. _____   _____   B. _____
   _____
   _____
   _____

C. _____   _____   C. _____
   _____
   _____
   _____
   _____

D. _____   _____   D. _____
   _____
   _____
   _____
   _____

E. _____   _____   E. _____
   _____
   _____
   _____
   _____

F. _____   _____   F. _____
   _____
   _____
   _____

G. _____   _____   G. _____
   _____
   _____
   _____

H. _____   _____   H. _____
   _____
   _____
   _____
   _____

STEP B

WEIGH ADVANTAGES OVER COMPETITORS

After you have assessed all the differences between your company and your competitors at each stage and function, you can begin to weigh existing and potential advantages (or disadvantages) related to each. Advantages exist when you do something better than your competitors do it, and they include a wide spectrum of possibilities, from doing things cheaper or faster to doing them with more quality control or precision. In the long run you want to understand the full value and significance of each advantage in the marketplace. If your customers don't perceive or value an advantage, it may not be an advantage after all. Have you misjudged the advantage? Can you find a way to persuade customers to value it?

In order to separate differences into advantages and disadvantages and to rank advantages according to their relative importance, you must become intimately familiar with every advantage or potential advantage competitors hold over one another in your industry. Such intimate knowledge requires an exhaustive and time-consuming search. As with differences, advantages can lie at any point on along the path of business stages or in any function, and some of them may be so subtle that you can find them only after intense analysis. So you must probe deeply to uncover all advantages, whether currently utilized or dormant, existing or potential.

Once you have listed and examined all advantages, you can judge their relative importance in the marketplace. How do customers value a particular advantage? The answer to this question will help you assign relative importance to each advantage. Since your company's strengths may make it more logical for you to exploit a certain advantage rather than another, you will eventually have to measure advantages against your company's strengths (the subject of the next chapter). But for now, Exercises 2 and 3 will help you evaluate differences and determine advantages.

EXERCISE 2
EVALUATING THE DIFFERENCES

Among the differences between your company and your competitors you will find both present and future competitive advantages and disadvantages. Before you begin Exercise 2, let's look at how our national discount-store chain performed its evaluation. On the surface many of the differences appeared to be negative, so the task force executives started by scrutinizing one of the obviously positive differences between their stores and their new competitor: national credit card program. The national chain's credit-card financing service served over 25 million customers nationwide and almost 1 million in this city alone.

EXERCISE 2 EXAMPLE

Major Differences from Exercise 1

A. Is the difference positive or negative?

B. What is the size or extent of the difference?

C. How long has the difference existed?

D. What caused the difference to develop and what customer need was it designed to fill?

E. How do customers perceive the difference?

F. How have competitors responded to the difference?

1. *National Credit Card Program*

   A. *Positive.*

   B. *Substantial, because the store's potential 1 million customers could charge up to $1,000 for merchandise on their credit cards.*

C. *Ever since the credit card program began ten years ago.*

D. *The store's goal of attracting the maximum number of customers. It fulfilled the need for customer purchases to be more convenient.*

E. *The 1 million customers who already held cards in the city perceived a major advantage.*

F. *A rumor is circulating that this competitor plans to offer a credit card to customers soon.*

As you complete Exercise 2, bear in mind that the thoroughness of your evaluation will greatly enhance the usefulness of future exercises in this chapter. Confine your analysis to the differences you labeled "major" in Exercise 1.

EXERCISE 2 WORKSHEET

Evaluating the Differences

Major Differences from Exercise 1

A. Is the difference positive or negative?
B. What is the size or extent of the difference?
C. How long has the difference existed?
D. What caused the difference to develop and what customer need was it designed to fill?
E. How do customers perceive the difference?
F. How have competitors responded to the difference?

1. _____

  A. _____

  B. _____

  C. _____

  D. _____

  E. _____

  F. _____

2. _____

  A. _____

  B. _____

  C. _____

  D. _____

  E. _____

  F. _____

3. _____

  A. _____

  B. _____

  C. _____

  D. _____

  E. _____

  F. _____

4. _____   A. _____
   _____   _____
   _____   _____

              B. _____
                 _____
                 _____

              C. _____
                 _____
                 _____

              D. _____
                 _____
                 _____

              E. _____
                 _____
                 _____

              F. _____
                 _____
                 _____

5. _____   A. _____
   _____   _____
   _____   _____

              B. _____
                 _____
                 _____

              C. _____
                 _____
                 _____

              D. _____
                 _____
                 _____

              E. _____
                 _____
                 _____

              F. _____
                 _____
                 _____

6. _____   A. _____
   _____   _____
   _____   _____

              B. _____
                 _____
                 _____

              C. _____
                 _____
                 _____

              D. _____
                 _____
                 _____

              E. _____
                 _____
                 _____

              F. _____
                 _____
                 _____

7. _____   A. _____
   _____   _____
   _____   _____

              B. _____
                 _____
                 _____

              C. _____
                 _____
                 _____

              D. _____
                 _____
                 _____

              E. _____
                 _____
                 _____

              F. _____
                 _____
                 _____

EXERCISE 2 WORKSHEET (*Cont.*)

8. _____ A. _____

9. _____ A. _____

    B. _____

    C. _____

    D. _____

    E. _____

    F. _____

9. _____ A. _____

    B. _____

    C. _____

    D. _____

    E. _____

F. _____

10. _____ A. _____

    B. _____

    C. _____

    D. _____

    E. _____

    F. _____

EXERCISE 3
DETERMINING THE ADVANTAGES

This exercise will help you determine which of the differences evaluated in Exercise 2 represent substantial competitive advantages for your company. Substantial advantages contain two basic elements: (1) the value customers place on a difference and (2) your competitor's ability to eliminate or neutralize the difference. In Exercise 3 you will contemplate these two elements with respect to the top ten differences ranked in Exercise 2.

The national chain determined that customers who currently held a credit-card placed a great deal of value on the line of credit behind it. After extensive interviews with customers, management concluded that the credit-card program had accumulated loyalty and trust among customers over the past ten years. The executives estimated that 300,000 customers in the local area used their cards frequently enough to perceive the service as very significant. In terms of their competitors' ability to eliminate this particular difference, the task force concluded that, for a majority of the 1 million credit-card holders in the surrounding metropolitan area, no competitor could eliminate the advantage in less than five years, and then only if the national chain did nothing to enhance its current position. For all practical purposes the ability of competitors to eliminate the advantage was "zero" over the short term.

EXERCISE 3 EXAMPLE

Difference #1: *National Credit-Card Program*

True Competitive Advantage: Yes __X__ No ____

Value to Customers: *Significant. We have enjoyed exceptionally high levels of customer loyalty because of our extensive credit-card financing services.*

Ability of Competitors to Eliminate: *None of our competitors can eliminate this advantage in the short term. A competitor could possibly*

duplicate what we have in five years, but if we keep improving our own credit card program the advantage will not be eliminated in the long term either.

As you write your own statements, remember that one customer segment may not value a given difference the same way another segment would. Therefore, you want to focus on segments that most highly value the difference. Also bear in mind that competitors may respond to a difference in varying ways. Concentrate on competitors who pose the greatest threats. When you finish your descriptions for each of the ten differences, review them in an effort to pinpoint true competitive advantages—differences highly valued by at least one customer segment and not easily erased by at least one major competitor.

EXERCISE 3 WORKSHEET

Determining the Advantages

Difference #1: _____

  True Competitive Advantage: Yes ____ No ____

  Value to Customers: _____

_____

_____

_____

  Ability of Competitors to Eliminate: _____

_____

_____

_____

Difference #2: _____

  True Competitive Advantage: Yes ____ No ____

  Value to Customers: _____

_____

_____

  Ability of Competitors to Eliminate: _____

_____

_____

_____

Difference #3: _____

  True Competitive Advantage: Yes ____ No ____

  Value to Customers: _____

_____

_____

_____

  Ability of Competitors to Eliminate: _____

_____

_____

_____

Difference #4: _____

  True Competitive Advantage: Yes ____ No ____

  Value to Customers: _____

_____

_____

_____

_____

  Ability of Competitors to Eliminate: _____

_____

_____

_____

Difference #5: _____

  True Competitive Advantage: Yes ____ No ____

  Value to Customers: _____

_____

_____

_____

  Ability of Competitors to Eliminate: _____

_____

_____

_____

Difference #6: _____

  True Competitive Advantage: Yes ____ No ____

  Value to Customers: _____

_____

_____

_____

  Ability of Competitors to Eliminate: _____

_____

_____

Difference #7: _____

  True Competitive Advantage: Yes ____ No ____

  Value to Customers: _____

_____

_____

_____

  Ability of Competitors to Eliminate: _____

_____

_____

_____

Difference #8: _____

   True Competitive Advantage: Yes ___ No ___

   Value to Customers: _____
_____
_____
_____
_____

   Ability of Competitors to Eliminate: _____
_____
_____
_____

Difference #9: _____

   True Competitive Advantage: Yes ___ No ___

   Value to Customers: _____
_____
_____
_____
_____

   Ability of Competitors to Eliminate: _____
_____
_____
_____

Difference #10: _____

   True Competitive Advantage: Yes ___ No ___

   Value to Customers: _____
_____
_____
_____

Ability of Competitors to Eliminate: _____
_____
_____
_____

STEP **C**

LOOK FOR SUSTAINABILITY OF ADVANTAGES

Sustainability refers to the long-term value of a particular advantage. Advantages you cannot maintain over the long term will never bring lasting success. Your assessment of sustainability must take into account the changes your industry will most likely experience, from changes in national or international tastes and trends to specific new programs or products offered by your competitors. A competitive advantage that appears sustainable now may later prove otherwise.

The best strategies demand long-term competitive advantages. If you cannot sustain a competitive advantage over the long term, you should question its value. If competitors can easily duplicate the advantage, or if customers will eventually ignore it, or if it requires an unacceptable level of effort and investment to maintain it, then you should look elsewhere for the edge that will set you apart from others. A short-term advantage may bring your company short-term profits, and you might briefly benefit from those gains, but a strategy based on short-term advantages will eventually run into trouble and force you into the almost impossible position of having to devise new short-term advantages year after year. Unfortunately, most companies that attempt a series of spectacular plays in favor of a complete game plan can only do so for a limited period of time, after which the ability to devise short-term advantages wanes or the opportunities for creating such "quick scores" disappear.

EXERCISE 4
ASSESSING SUSTAINABILITY

In this exercise you will assess whether or not you can sustain the true competitive advantages identified in Exercise 3. No matter how much you prize a particular advantage, it does not deserve a role in your long-range strategy unless you can maintain it over the years.

As the task force of the national chain considered the sustainability of its credit-card advantage, for example, it determined that the company could maintain that edge for five years without much effort, but after that the advantage would decline as rivals implemented their own programs. Therefore the task force concluded that the chain would have to enhance its credit-card program gradually over the next five years.

Competitive Advantages in Order of Importance	A. Expected duration (years). B. How will you sustain the advantage? C. Can you enhance the advantage? How? D. How will competitors respond to your efforts? E. What unforeseen events could erase this advantage in ten years?
1. *National Credit-Card Program*	A. *Five years.* B. *By expanding on our current program.* C. *Yes. Through raising credit limits, offering checking and savings services, and installing ATM's.* D. *They will attempt to duplicate our credit-card program.* E. *The total and complete deregulation of the financial services industry would make it easier to duplicate our program.*

To make sure you confront the issue of sustainability head on, apply the following sustainability test to all your truly competitive advantages.

EXERCISE 4 WORKSHEET

Assessing Sustainability

Competitive Advantages in Order of Importance

A. Expected duration (years).
B. How will you sustain the advantage?
C. Can you enhance the advantage? How?
D. How will competitors respond to your efforts?
E. What unforeseen events could erase this advantage in ten years?

1. _____

   _____

   _____

   A. _____

   _____

   B. _____

   _____

   _____

   _____

   C. _____

   _____

   _____

   _____

   D. _____

   _____

   _____

   _____

   E. _____

   _____

   _____

   _____

   _____

   _____

2. _____

   _____

   _____

   A. _____

   _____

   B. _____

   _____

   _____

   _____

   _____

   C. _____

   _____

   _____

   D. _____

   _____

   _____

   _____

   E. _____

   _____

   _____

   _____

   _____

   _____

3. _____

   _____

   _____

   A. _____

   _____

   B. _____

   _____

   _____

   _____

   C. _____

   _____

   _____

   _____

   D. _____

   _____

   _____

   _____

4. _____

    E. _____

    A. _____

    B. _____

    C. _____

    D. _____

    E. _____

5. _____

    A. _____

    B. _____

    C. _____

6. _____

    D. _____

    E. _____

    A. _____

    B. _____

    C. _____

    D. _____

    E. _____

SUMMARY

You should now record all your conclusions from each of the exercises. Review each one carefully, then summarize the most important ones under "Overall Summary of Conclusions." Don't forget to spend some time brainstorming about future directions you might take to create a sustained competitive advantage.

Below is a sampling of the national chain task force's conclusions.

SUMMARY WORKSHEET

PART A

Conclusions from Step A, Exercise 1, pages 34–41

1. _____
_____
_____
_____
_____

2. _____
_____
_____
_____
_____

3. _____
_____
_____
_____
_____

PART B

Conclusions from Step B, Exercises 2 and 3, pages 44–49

1. _____
_____
_____
_____

2. _____
_____
_____
_____

3. _____
_____
_____
_____

PART C

Conclusions from Step C, Exercise 4, pages 52–53

1. _____
_____
_____
_____

2. _____
_____
_____
_____

3. _____
_____
_____
_____

PART D

Overall Summary of Conclusions

1. _____
_____
_____
_____

2. _____
_____
_____

3. _____
_____
_____

4. _____
_____
_____

SUMMARY WORKSHEET (*Cont.*)

5. _____
_____
_____
_____
_____
_____

6. _____
_____
_____
_____
_____

PART E
Future Directions

_____
_____
_____
_____
_____
_____
_____
_____
_____
_____
_____
_____
_____
_____
_____
_____

Successful strategists think long term. You may satisfy customer needs for a time, but your tough competitors will always be searching for ways to beat you at it. To continue satisfying customers and sustaining competitive advantages, you must be able to marshal your company's strengths behind your goals. If your strategy depends on a big difference between your company and your competitors, but does not spring from a solid company strength, the strategy will inevitably fail. In the next chapter you will complete your assessment of long-range strategy by looking more closely at your organization's strengths.

CHAPTER 3

CAPITALIZING ON COMPANY STRENGTHS

The Foothill Group, recognizing a need to diversify away from commercial financing, decided to get into oil field equipment leasing because it assumed its financial expertise could help it profit from such a special market. However, Foothill lacked the skills required to successfully lease oil field equipment. It didn't require adequate collateral from borrowers, and it couldn't cope with an unexpected equipment market slump. Although Foothill executives initially calculated that they could capitalize on a proven strength, they soon learned they didn't really understand their strengths, particularly when directed toward a new market.

When a company embarks upon a strategy that does not capitalize on existing strengths, the strategy almost always fails. Fifty years ago you might have been able to enter a new market with few relevant strengths and succeed by virtue of your ideas and hard work, but today's tough competitive markets, where companies have finely honed their strengths, demand more than innovation and determination. Strategies built upon nonexistent strengths are like houses built on sand—they crumble under pressure.

Assuming you have found new ways to satisfy customer needs and sustain competitive advantages, you must determine whether your company has sufficient strengths to implement your plans. If not, you should pause to consider whether or not you can acquire or build the necessary strengths fast enough and thoroughly enough to succeed. All too often executives feel optimistic about their abilities to make quick, dramatic changes despite the fact that the history of corporate failures indicates the hazard of such optimism.

Toro, the lawnmower and snowblower maker, launched a strategy that, by ignoring its strengths, resulted in staggering losses and a massive layoff. Two of the company's strengths, product quality and a faithful dealer network, had led the company to record sales of $400 million a few years ago, but then Toro changed to a marketing strategy that depended on mass merchandisers. At the same time, management speeded up the product development process to take advantage of a growing market. The mass merchandisers undercut Toro's traditional hardware store dealers, who, stung by this insensitivity to their loyalty, began jumping ship, and the shortened product development cycle caused product quality to slide. The end result was a $13 million loss, the company's first, on a drop in sales of 38 percent in 1981. Toro's top management resigned and over 2,000 workers lost their jobs. Having ignored the hard-won strengths of product quality and faithful dealers, Toro has found the road back to be painfully slow, earning only $8 million on sales of $280 million in 1984.

In contrast, Progresso Quality Food Company has long promoted the fresh, quality ingredients of its soups and sauces. The resultant image of quality has allowed the company to grow from a small producer of specialty Italian foods to a $240 million gourmet and ethnic food producer. Building on one of its key strengths, quality ingredients, Progresso began courting segments of Campbell Soup's market, and in New York and Boston eventually established a lead over Campbell's Chunky Soups with its own sixteen varieties of ready-to-serve soups. Not many companies would compete directly with a giant like Campbell, but as Campbell's marketing vice president, Herbert Baum, told *Business Week*, "They [Progresso] know how to make good soup and market well." Those are flattering words from one's archcompetitor. In fact, Progresso's focus on producing the most authentic ethnic products with superior quality displays all the characteristics of a brilliant strategy. Rather than engage Campbell in a head-to-head battle, Progresso set its sights on the needs of gourmet and ethnic customers, thus stealing away previously underserved segments. Quality ingredients really matter to such customers.

To capitalize on company strengths you must take three important steps:

Step A: *Measure resources*
Step B: *Understand strengths*
Step C: *Forecast exploitability of strengths*

As do customers and competitors, resources and assets also change. You must continually measure and evaluate your strengths, always directing them behind a strategy that fully exploits them in the evolving marketplace.

STEP A

MEASURE RESOURCES

First, you must identify all the resources resident in your company. Resources fall into two categories: means or assets and abilities or talents. Organizations invest both means and abilities to accomplish their goals, and while you'll find it harder to quantify abilities than means, you must inventory them all, whether you currently employ them or not. Since both types of resources form the basis for all company strengths, you must learn to "think resources" before attempting to capitalize on them. Company means or assets can be financial, technological, physical, or people-related, while company abilities or talents can include marketing know-how, distribution savvy, quality control, reputation for service, technological innovativeness, and entrepreneurship. Since a given resource may not necessarily be a strength, never confuse the two. True, strengths do grow out of resources, but resources alone do not produce strengths. Only action can do that.

EXERCISE 1
INVENTORYING COMPANY MEANS/ASSETS

Your company possesses both major and minor means to accomplish various goals. Before you can determine your strengths, you must understand these means, not all of which are immediately obvious.

By way of illustration, consider the case of a major city newspaper. The newspaper began scrutinizing its future by hiring a consultant who specialized in competitive strategy. The consultant guided the paper's top management team through a series of analytical exercises in an effort to identify some basic strengths the paper could further exploit.

When, five years earlier, the paper had drastically overhauled its long-standing format and design, the change had at first bothered many employees, who saw no reason to tamper with a format that had been so successful in the past. The company had a long history of profitability and operated with almost no debt on its balance sheet. But a new executive editor, the paper's former art director, had been determined to inject a new attitude of creativity and experimentation into the paper, and before long his spirit of innovation began to spread throughout most departments. Two years after the new editor took over, he utilized some of the company's financial resources to invest in the latest printing technology, including a sophisticated computer graphics system in keeping with the company's growing innovative style.

When polled about the flashy new format and orientation, the paper's subscribers fell into two camps. Older, more conservative subscribers, fearing the paper was compromising its journalistic reputation by placing too much emphasis on image, design, and packaging, tended to disapprove. However, younger subscribers, ages twenty-five to forty, welcomed the sleeker look. Since younger subscribers composed the largest and fastest-growing segment of the market, the paper's management congratulated itself on having achieved a competitive advantage over a rival paper that still clung to journalistic arrogance. Its publisher had even gone so far as to say, "Our competition places more emphasis on marketing than on reporting." After the controversy died down, the innovative paper eventually took its format and orientation for granted.

The paper's top management began its exploration of strengths by constructing an inventory based on the consultant's suggestion that they divide their discussion of resources into two parts: means and abilities. The newspaper executives identified four primary and two secondary means:

EXERCISE 1 EXAMPLE

Company Means	Do You Enjoy This Means?	Primary/ Secondary
Profit/ Retained Earnings	X	*Primary*
Debit Capacity	X	*Secondary*
Cash/ Securities	X	*Primary*
Reputation/ Image	X	*Primary*
Customer Loyalty	X	*Primary*
Technology	X	*Secondary*

As you perform this exercise, place an X next to each of the means your company enjoys. Then determine whether it is primary or secondary. By primary we mean that it relates directly to your ability to satisfy customers and compete effectively against your rivals, and by secondary we mean that it only tangentially or indirectly does so.

Inventorying Company Means/Assets

Company Means	Do You Enjoy This Means?	Primary/Secondary
Profit/Retained Earnings		
Debt Capacity		
Established Credit Line		
Cash and Securities		
Other Financial Means		
Production Facilities		
Materials Handling Equipment		
Distribution Equipment		
Other Plant and Equipment		
Reputation/Image		
Customer Loyalty		
Customer Contracts		
Dealer Network		
Other Marketing Means		
Natural Resources		
Supplier Agreements		
Other Supply Means		
Operations Personnel		
Financial Personnel		
Marketing Personnel		
Sales Personnel		
Management Personnel		
Other Personnel		
Technology		
Patents		
Legal Protection		
Licenses		
Other Unusual Advantages		
Other Means:		

EXERCISE 2
UNCOVERING COMPANY ABILITIES/TALENTS

This exercise will help you identify abilities and talents. Company abilities are the things your company knows how to do. Major abilities relate directly to satisfying customers and competing effectively, while minor ones do so only indirectly.

The newspaper company's management team uncovered five important abilities.

EXERCISE 2 EXAMPLE

Company Abilities	Do You Possess This Ability?	Primary/ Secondary
Innovativeness	X	*Primary*
Entrepreneurship	X	*Primary*
New Product Development	X	*Secondary*
Marketing Prowess	X	*Primary*
Internal Communications Ability	X	*Secondary*

As you did in Exercise 1, try to go beyond the most obvious abilities to the less obvious or even dormant ones. Identify as many abilities as you can.

Uncovering Company Abilities/Talents

Company Abilities	Do You Possess This Ability?	Primary/Secondary
Innovativeness	_____	_____
New Product Development	_____	_____
Creativity	_____	_____
Entrepreneurship	_____	_____
Technical Know-how	_____	_____
Financial Adeptness	_____	_____
Operations Capability	_____	_____
Supplier Relationships Effectiveness	_____	_____
Marketing Prowess	_____	_____
Sales Talent	_____	_____
Distribution Ability	_____	_____
Customer Service Effectiveness	_____	_____
Customer Relations Proficiency	_____	_____
Legal Savvy	_____	_____
Productivity	_____	_____
Cost Control	_____	_____
Organizational Effectiveness	_____	_____
Responsiveness to Change	_____	_____
Systems Efficiency	_____	_____
Management Aptitude	_____	_____
Internal Communications Ability	_____	_____
External Communications Ability	_____	_____
People Development Ability	_____	_____
Rewards and Compensation Success	_____	_____
Strategic and Organizational Analysis	_____	_____
Decision-Making Ability	_____	_____
Problem-Solving Ability	_____	_____
Conflict-Resolution Ability	_____	_____
Other Abilities	_____	_____
_____	_____	_____
_____	_____	_____
_____	_____	_____
_____	_____	_____
_____	_____	_____
_____	_____	_____
_____	_____	_____
_____	_____	_____
_____	_____	_____
_____	_____	_____
_____	_____	_____
_____	_____	_____

UNDERSTAND STRENGTHS

Following a complete inventory of resources, you can undertake a determination of strengths. By strengths we mean the active combination of means and abilities to accomplish objectives. Unutilized resources or insufficient matching of means with abilities are not strengths, because strengths exist only when you match the means to do something with the ability to do it.

If the combination of a means and an ability produces superior results compared to competitors, companies in other industries, or other departments within your own company, then you can judge the combination a genuine strength. When Apple Computer utilized its financial means to develop a brand-new kind of computer and combined it with superior engineering and technological know-how, the result was a genuine strength and a new machine, the Macintosh. Exxon used its vast financial means to get into the office systems business but lacked the ability to manage that kind of business. The result was not a strength but a disaster.

As in sports, mere size alone does not guarantee a champion; a smaller but more agile competitor who understands speed, agility, and leverage will often triumph over a muscle-bound opponent.

EXERCISE 3
DETERMINING COMPANY STRENGTHS

Now you can begin matching means with abilities to produce strengths. At the beginning of the exercise list all your primary means and abilities (secondary means and abilities seldom combine by themselves to produce substantial strengths). With these lists in hand, you can begin patiently meditating on the existing or potential relationships among them. Ask yourself, "Has this means and this ability combined to create a strength in the past? If not, could they in the future?" If you answer yes, record the match under "combinations," adding a brief description of what results the combination has produced in the past or might produce in the future. If you answer no, then consider another combination. Note that more than one means and more than one ability can combine to create a strength, so try to consider all the many possible combinations.

The newspaper executives decided one of the company's genuine strengths was "Newspaper Design and Concept Innovation." Their chart looked like the example on the facing page.

EXERCISE 3 EXAMPLE

**Primary Means
(From Exercise 1)**

1. *Profit/Retained Earnings*
2. *Reputation/Image*
3. *Customer Loyalty*

**Primary Abilities
(From Exercise 2)**

1. *Innovativeness*
2. *Entrepreneurship*
3. *Marketing Prowess*

Secondary Means

1. *Debt Capacity*
2. *Cash/Securities*
3. *Technology*

Secondary Abilities

1. *New Product Testing*
2. *Internal Communications*

Once the newspaper executives had summarized their findings from Exercises 1 and 2, they began mentally combining means and abilities to discover the real strengths of the company. After some discussion and numerous combinations they agreed on a set of company strengths. The combination of means and abilities that created one of these strengths is outlined in the example below:

Company Strength: *Newspaper Design and Concept Innovation*

Means: *Profit/Retained Earnings, Debt Capacity, Reputation/Image, Technology*

Abilities: *Innovativeness, Entrepreneurship, Marketing Prowess*

Results of Combination and Why It Produced Strength: *The unique combination of financial means and innovative abilities led to the development of an important strength related to the design and concept of the newspaper. The strength came about because we supported innovation with adequate funding.*

As you complete this exercise, take your time. Trying to hurry may result in an ill-defined strength with insufficient understanding of its roots. If you don't truly understand a company strength and its makeup, you will not be able to fully exploit it later.

Determining Company Strengths

Primary Means (From Exercise 1)	Primary Abilities (From Exercise 2)	Secondary Means	Secondary Abilities
1. _____	1. _____	1. _____	1. _____
2. _____	2. _____	2. _____	2. _____
3. _____	3. _____	3. _____	3. _____
4. _____	4. _____	4. _____	4. _____
5. _____	5. _____	5. _____	5. _____
6. _____	6. _____	6. _____	6. _____
7. _____	7. _____	7. _____	7. _____
8. _____	8. _____	8. _____	8. _____
9. _____	9. _____	9. _____	9. _____
10. _____	10. _____	10. _____	10. _____

Company Strength	A. Primary Means/ Secondary Means	B. Primary Abilities/ Secondary Abilities

C. Results of Combination and Why It Produced Strength

1. _____ A. _____ B. _____
   _____   _____   _____
                     _____   _____
                     _____   _____
                     _____   _____

C. _____
_____
_____
_____
_____
_____
_____

2. _____ A. _____ B. _____
   _____   _____   _____
                     _____   _____
                     _____   _____

C.

3.   **A.**   **B.**

C.

4.   **A.**   **B.**

C.

5.   **A.**   **B.**

C.

EXERCISE 3 WORKSHEET (*Cont.*)

6. _____ A. _____ B. _____
   _____   _____   _____
                                 _____   _____
                                 _____   _____
                                 _____

C. _____
   _____
   _____
   _____
   _____
   _____
   _____
   _____

7. _____ A. _____ B. _____
   _____   _____   _____
                                 _____   _____
                                 _____   _____
                                 _____

C. _____
   _____
   _____
   _____
   _____
   _____
   _____
   _____

8. _____ A. _____ B. _____
   _____   _____   _____
                                 _____   _____
                                 _____   _____
                                 _____

C. _____
   _____
   _____
   _____
   _____
   _____
   _____

RANKING COMPANY STRENGTHS

In this exercise you will rank the strengths identified in Exercise 3. To do so, you will compare each one to similar strengths (or weaknesses) among competitors, companies in related industries, and other departments within your own company. Although any such rating involves a great deal of subjectivity, the process of carefully detailing the reasons behind your ratings should make your strategic thinking as objective as possible. To accomplish the rating of each strength we suggest you use a scale of 1 to 10, (10 = clearly better than others, 9–7 = somewhat better, 6–4 = about the same, 3–1 = clearly worse). The purpose of this exercise is to rank company strengths by totaling your ratings in each of the three areas mentioned above and then using the total score to rank the importance of each of the strengths.

The newspaper executives awarded a 10 to "Newspaper Design and Concept Innovation" in all three areas of comparison for a total of 30, clearly winning that strength a #1 ranking. Had the executives been asked about its relative importance before they undertook this exercise, they would have ranked it behind several others. The newspaper's second-ranked strength, "Feature Article Quality and Depth," won a 25 (9, 7, and 9) rating total.

EXERCISE 4 EXAMPLE

Company Strength	Against Competitors?	Against Companies In Related Industries?	Against Other Department Strengths?	Total
1. *Newspaper Design and Concept Innovation*	10	10	10	30

Reasons: *Compared to competitors, magazine publishers, and other departments here, our strength in design and concept innovation is unparalleled.*

Company Strength	Against Competitors?	Against Companies In Related Industries?	Against Other Department Strengths?	Total
2. *Feature Article Quality and Depth*	9	7	9	25

Reasons: *Against competitors our paper is somewhat better in this area. Relative to companies in related industries, particularly magazine publishers, our feature articles are slightly better. And, compared to other department strengths in our own company, most other strengths rate a 7 or lower.*

Spend some time pondering the reasons behind your ratings. To test the validity of your ratings, instruct each member of your management team to complete Exercise 4 separately, then compare them all. The consolidation of all ratings, possibly tossing out the highest and lowest scores, will reduce subjectivity.

EXERCISE 4 WORKSHEET

Ranking Company Strengths

Strength	Against Competitors?	Against Companies In Related Industries?	Against Other Department Strengths?	Total

1. _____ _____ _____ _____ _____

Reasons: _____

_____
_____
_____
_____
_____
_____
_____
_____

2. _____ _____ _____ _____ _____

Reasons: _____

_____
_____
_____
_____
_____
_____
_____
_____
_____
_____
_____
_____

3. _____ _____ _____ _____ _____

Reasons: _____

_____
_____
_____
_____
_____
_____
_____
_____
_____
_____

4. _____

Reasons: _____

_____

_____

_____

_____

_____

_____

_____

5. _____

Reasons: _____

_____

_____

_____

_____

_____

_____

_____

_____

6. _____

Reasons: _____

_____

_____

_____

_____

_____

_____

_____

STEP C

FORECAST EXPLOITABILITY OF STRENGTHS

Finally, you can begin to predict the exploitability of your company strengths. Exploitability depends both on your current allocation of strengths and on how you might further allocate them in the future.

Since successful strategies depend on the optimum deployment of strengths, you must gain a thorough understanding of your current position before weighing opportunities for enhancing your position. If a company strength offers substantial opportunities for further exploitation or is currently underutilized, this fact should help dictate any new direction. By the same token, wise executives remain ever wary of apparent strengths that actually do little to meet customer needs or sustain competitive advantage. Currently unexploited company strengths, like unsatisfied customer needs and undeveloped competitive advantages, offer great opportunities for future strategies.

EXERCISE 5
ASSESSING EXPLOITABILITY

This exercise will enable you to assess the exploitability of your top six strengths. It involves:

1. Assessing current levels of exploitation
2. Assessing opportunities for further exploitation
3. Identifying methods for further exploitation

Rate each of the first two items as High, Medium, or Low (for further refinement you can add a + or −), then describe specific methods by which you could extend each strength. You make such an evaluation by simultaneously considering current and future exploitability. For example, if there are substantial opportunities for further exploitation of a strength, it probably deserves a "High" rating. In conjunction with this "High" rating for further exploitation probably comes a "Medium" or "Low" rating for current exploitation. However, if the opportunites for exploitation of a strength are enormous you may find yourself rating both current exploitation and further exploitation as "High."

The newspaper executives concluded that the current level of exploitation of "Newspaper Design and Concept Innovation" deserved a "Medium +" and the opportunites for further exploitation a "High," and that they could "further exploit the strength by diversifying into related industries such as magazine and book publishing."

Strength

1. *Newspaper Design and Concept Innovation*
   A. Current Level of Exploitation:
      Medium +
   B. Opportunities for Further Exploitation:
      High

C. Methods for Further Exploitation:
Diversity into other publishing fields such as magazine or book publishing

    Again, encourage each person on your management team to complete Exercise 5 separately, then merge their individual results to arrive at the most objective consensus.

EXERCISE 5 WORKSHEET

Assessing Exploitability

STRENGTH

    A. Current Level of Exploitation
       High   Medium   Low

    B. Opportunites for Further Exploitation
       High   Medium   Low

C. Methods for Further Exploitation

1. _____
   A. _____
   B. _____

    C. _____

2. _____
   A. _____
   B. _____

    C. _____

3. _____
   A. _____
   B. _____

    C. _____

4. _____
   A. _____
   B. _____

    C. _____

5. _____

    A. _____

    B. _____

C. _____

_____

_____

_____

_____

_____

_____

6. _____

    A. _____

    B. _____

C. _____

_____

_____

_____

_____

_____

_____

SUMMARY

After developing conclusions from each set of exercises, write an overall summary of the conclusions.

Below is a sampling of the newspaper's conclusions.

SUMMARY EXAMPLE

PART A

Conclusions from Step A, Exercises 1 and 2

The financial means of our company seem much more impressive and powerful than we imagined.

PART B

Conclusions from Step B, Exercises 3 and 4

Rather than rest on our laurels in the area of Design and Concept Innovation, we should find ways to further exploit this "#1" strength.

PART C

Conclusions from Step C, Exercise 5

We need to become very aggressive about looking for acquisition opportunities in our own and related industries.

PART D

Overall Summary of Conclusions

Our design and concept uniqueness is sufficiently advantageous to warrant expansion through acquisition of other newspapers and possibly related businesses.

PART E

Future Directions

We might experiment with using our design and concept strengths by offering a topical monthly magazine on local newsmakers, some sort of local People *magazine; or by publishing a book with a pictorial account of our university's championship football season.*

SUMMARY WORKSHEET

PART A

Conclusions from Step A, Exercises 1 and 2, pages 61–63

1. _____
_____
_____
_____

2. _____
_____
_____
_____

3. _____
_____
_____
_____

PART B

Conclusions from Step B, Exercises 3 and 4, pages 66–71

1. _____
_____
_____
_____

2. _____
_____
_____
_____

3. _____
_____
_____

PART C

Conclusions from Step C, Exercise 5, pages 74–75

1. _____
_____
_____
_____
_____

2. _____
_____
_____
_____

3. _____
_____
_____
_____

1. _____
_____
_____
_____
_____

2. _____
_____
_____
_____

3. _____
_____
_____
_____

PART D

Overall Summary of Conclusions

1. _____
_____
_____

SUMMARY WORKSHEET (*Cont.*)

2. _____
_____
_____

3. _____
_____
_____
_____

4. _____
_____
_____

5. _____
_____
_____
_____

6. _____
_____
_____
_____

PART E

Future Directions

_____
_____
_____
_____
_____
_____
_____

_____
_____
_____
_____
_____
_____
_____
_____
_____
_____
_____

At this point you have finished your assessment of the strategy half of your strategy-culture alloy and can now turn to a penetrating audit of your corporate culture.

No matter how wisely you have decided to better satisfy customer needs, win greater advantages over your competitors, and more productively employ your strengths, your strategy will not create lasting excellence unless you build a culture capable of carrying it out with commitment, competence, and consistency. In the next three chapters, you will carefully analyze the three essential ingredients in a strong culture; then, in Chapter 7, you will assemble all you have learned into a sweeping picture of where your strategy-culture alloy might take you.

CHAPTER 4

CULTIVATING COMMITMENT TO A COMMON PURPOSE

Bill Marshall, president of the Shawmut Bank—Worcester Group, had brought his senior executives together at the beautiful Rockefeller-owned Woodstock Inn in Vermont. By giving his key people and their spouses some company-paid recreation time in a luxury resort, Marshall hoped to convey his appreciation for an outstanding year. In 1984 the Worcester Group, which accounted for over one-fifth of Shawmut's $6 billion in assets, had paved the way toward record earnings with a fine financial performance. Before turning everyone loose for recreation, Marshall led them through an intense two-day marathon of presentations, analysis, and discussion that he hoped would unite them behind a central vision, an undertaking Marshall thought crucial given Shawmut's recent history of acquisitions and reorganizations. Two years earlier, Shawmut of Boston had acquired Worcester Bancorp, which, prior to the merger with Shawmut, had itself completed a string of acquisitions. As a result, 1984 had been a year of crisis management, with the twelve Shawmut-Worcester executives, under Marshall's direction, spending a great deal of time putting out fires, softening the culture shock of merger and

reorganization upheavals, and solidifying the Worcester Group's financial position.

At the meeting in Vermont, in late January 1985, Marshall wanted to turn everyone's attention to the company's future. Rather than impose his own vision on the group, he wisely chose to involve his key people in the process of developing one, thereby ensuring their full commitment. During the work session the Shawmut executive team followed many of the steps presented in this chapter, and when they adjourned they felt the beginnings of a fresh sense of excitement over their future. They had developed a deeper understanding of the common purpose of their company by debating strategy and culture issues at length, and as a result reached a budding consensus about the bank's direction. Of course they didn't cement commitment to a common purpose during a few scant days in Vermont, but they did lay the foundation.

Why do some executives, like Bill Marshall, work so hard to imbue their organizations with a commitment to a common purpose? Quite simply, such executives are aware of the crucial role commitment plays in building a strong corporate culture. Too many executives immerse themselves so deeply in the mechanics of their businesses that the details drown the fundamental principles that spur people to accomplish extraordinary feats. No fundamental principle should preoccupy executives more than developing commitment to a common mission. Such dedication results in "people power," the strongest force any organization can hope to harness.

Dravo Corporation, an engineering and construction firm that just a few years ago seemed destined for eminence, recently lost sight of this principle and began floundering. From $1.4 billion in revenues in 1983, sales in 1984 plummeted 40 percent, and the company suffered an $11.2 million operating loss. *Business Week* reported the astonishment of Dravo's competitors at how quickly the empire had crumbled. What happened? Or more to the point, what *didn't* happen? Despite installing a new CEO, Thomas Faught, in 1982, Dravo could not resolve a crisis that had begun to materialize much earlier. Like most of its competitors, Dravo struggled with the recession and key management changes, but, unlike some of them, Dravo couldn't cope with the crises. Thus, while some engineering and construction companies with strong commitments to their missions responded creatively to the market conditions, Dravo executives and employees, lacking a clear mission, were paralyzed. When the recession wound down in the early 1980s, Dravo's people stood ready and willing to embrace the future, but Faught and his executive group remained silent. No vision emerged. Left in the dark about the company's mission, employees grew discouraged and disorganized, until many began looking elsewhere for jobs. Two years without a unifying purpose can kill a company. *The Wall Street Journal* recently reported that Dravo has finally begun to rally around a new vision, but the two-year drought will be very hard to overcome.

In another industry besieged by change, Ron Stegall, senior vice president of Tandy's business products, has paid attention to the fundamental task of rallying his troops behind a compelling new vision. Tandy Corporation, the electronics and computer company, has also suffered declining earnings, but, unlike Dravo, it did not just sit on its hands waiting for a miracle. Instead, Stegall began attacking the fragmented, underserved small-business market, where success would depend on Tandy's people becoming much more aggressive, bucking their company's traditional passive sales approach. Tandy's salespeople learned what their products could and couldn't do, got to know certain targeted businesses intimately, and then went out to call on and educate those prospective customers. They couldn't wait for advertising to lure customers through the door.

Stegall's own enthusiasm for this new thrust has infected his people, because he has taken time to hire the right people and discuss issues thoroughly enough with them to produce a consensus. And he backs it all up with increased sales training and innovative computer lessons for customers. Although results may come slowly in this fiercely competitive industry, Stegall's people won't be wringing their hands or marching off in different directions. Perhaps he'll eventually duplicate his earlier success, when, as head of computer marketing, he pushed sales to schools from $6 million to over $100 million. Regardless, Stegall knows the value of commitment to a common purpose.

To cultivate commitment to a common purpose in your own organization you must take three fundamental steps:

Step A: *Articulate your company's common purpose*

Step B: *Determine level of commitment*

Step C: *Assess the degree to which commitment creates excellence*

By the end of this process, you will have arrived at the sort of purpose or mission statement to which you and your people can wholeheartedly commit yourselves.

STEP A

ARTICULATE YOUR COMPANY'S COMMON PURPOSE

First you must clarify and then state your company's purpose, mission, or vision in a powerful way. The best statement is both simple and subtle—simple enough for everyone to easily understand and embrace, subtle enough to contain rich implications for each and every member of the organization. It should answer four basic questions: What? How? Why? With what results?

- **What?** What goals do we actually want to accomplish? What image do we wish to project and support? What distinguishes our products and services?

- **How?** How will we accomplish our goals and win a sustained competitive advantage?

- **Why?** Why are we trying to accomplish our goals? Why will our people work to achieve superior performances?

- **Results?** In what measurable ways will our customers benefit? In what measurable ways will our employees benefit?

Notice the emphasis on *supporting* as well as *projecting* a purpose and image. If you don't base your mission on an honest, substantial belief and effort, your customers, competitors, and employees will quickly penetrate the public relations hype.

A large chemical company answered the four basic questions with the following mission statement:

Use our company's hard-won, respected expertise in efficiently manufacturing chemicals to become and remain the low-cost producer for every product by selecting high-volume products, constructing and operating highly efficient facilities, and stressing product dependability over product differentiation. This will minimize customers' costs, ensure their loyalty, and bring our company and its people the benefits of sustained growth and profitability.

What goals does the company want to accomplish? "Become and remain the low-cost producer for every product." *How* will it do this? "By selecting high-volume products, constructing and operating highly efficient facilities, and stressing product dependability over product differentiation." *Why* will people work hard to reach the goals? "Because they have worked hard to build our company's hard-won, respected expertise in efficiently manufacturing chemicals, which has brought them the benefits of growth and profitability." And, finally, what *results* can the company expect? "Minimize customers' costs, ensure their loyalty, and bring our company and its people the benefits of sustained growth and profitability."

No matter how you phrase your own statement, it must capture the *essence* of your organization. As with the components of your strategy, you should "think purpose," which, of course, derives from the underlying thrust of your strategy. What lies at the heart of your company's strategy?

A powerful mission statement must also be durable enough to withstand the changes, both anticipated and unforeseen, that any organization inevitably experiences. Since it takes time for everyone in an organization to develop a common commitment, the best mission statement can remain unchanged even though, over time, new strategies propel the company in different directions. IBM's customer service orientation has stood the test of time for over fifty years. Your purpose should ring true for a minimum of ten years.

EXERCISE 1
DEFINING YOUR PURPOSE

By the end of this exercise you will have defined the basic elements of your company's purpose or mission statement. Before you can write a simple yet subtle one, you must answer the four basic questions: What? How? Why? With what results? Because your answers should spring naturally from your company's strategy, you might begin by reviewing the conclusions you drew at the end of Chapters 1, 2, and 3.

A well-known computer company's executives reviewed their strategy before they attempted to state their company's mission. We'll call the company JCN. When they had considered the ways in which JCN satisfied customer needs, management concluded that their prime targets were sophisticated customers with highly technical needs who demanded state-of-the-art equipment for applications in aerospace engineering, nuclear power plant design, and telecommunications. To meet these needs, JCN had to stay on the leading edge of hardware and software design technology and had to field a sales and service force that could talk the language of technically sophisticated customers.

To sustain competitive advantage, JCN could rely on the fact that its scientists and engineers held more patents for advanced hardware and software products than any other firm in the industry. Furthermore, it recruited people with strong science and engineering backgrounds into its sales and service staffs. Finally, JCN could capitalize on its strengths by extending its engineering prowess, as well as its effective recruitment and training techniques.

Keeping their conclusions about strategy in mind, JCN's executives turned to answering the four questions every good mission statement must answer: What? How? Why? Results?

EXERCISE 1 EXAMPLE

1. *What? What goals do we actually want to accomplish? What image do we wish to project and support? What distinguishes our products and services?*

We want to be the technology leader. We wish to project and support an image of technical engineering prowess and informed sales and service representation to our sophisticated customers. Our products and services are distinguished by technical superiority.

2. *How? How will we accomplish our goals and win a sustained competitive advantage?*

We will stress hardware and software innovations and knowledgeable presentations of those innovations to our highly technical, engineering-oriented customers.

3. *Why? Why are we trying to accomplish our goals? Why will our people work to achieve superior performances?*

We are in business to innovate at the forefront of computer technology, an undertaking of great importance to the scientific and engineering community. We intend to maintain our position for the next twenty-five years and beyond for the benefit of our people and customers.

4. *Results? In what measurable ways will our customers benefit? In what measurable ways will our employees benefit?*

Our innovations will assist our customers in achieving their own breakthroughs, thereby enabling our own people to benefit from both the satisfaction and the financial rewards of enhancing our customers' accomplishments.

As you proceed to answer these questions for your own company, remember that you are looking for answers that will endure for ten or more years. As your company grows your strategies may change, but your mission or common purpose must be able to encompass those changes.

EXERCISE 1 WORKSHEET

Defining Your Purpose

1. What? What goals do we actually want to accomplish? What image do we wish to project and support? What distinguishes our products and services?

_____
_____
_____
_____
_____
_____
_____
_____

2. How? How will we accomplish our goals and win a sustained competitive advantage?

_____
_____
_____
_____
_____
_____
_____
_____

3. Why? Why are we trying to accomplish our goals? Why will our people work to achieve superior performance?

_____
_____
_____
_____
_____
_____
_____
_____

4. Results? In what measurable ways will our customers benefit? In what measurable ways will our employees benefit?

_____
_____
_____
_____
_____
_____
_____
_____

EXERCISE 2
STATING YOUR PURPOSE OR MISSION

Now you want to convert your answers into powerful statements you can weave together into one compelling mission statement, ultimately no longer than one clear, meaningful sentence.

How did JCN blend its four answers into one statement? As usually happens, it took a few tries before the executives felt they had satisfied the criteria of simplicity and subtlety.

Version #5 (**Final**):

We will knowledgeably deliver the most innovative and advanced computer technology to technically sophisticated customers, thereby supporting our customers' own innovations and providing our people with the satisfaction and financial rewards of enhancing our customers' accomplishments.

On the worksheet you will find spaces for up to five versions of your own mission statement. A famous philosopher once sent a long letter to a friend, apologizing that "I would have made it shorter, but I didn't have the time." Since it does take time to find just the right words to express your thoughts clearly and succinctly, painstakingly revise and polish your final statement. Your team won't remember or relate to a long-winded one, and they won't agree on the meaning of a cryptic one. Answer the four basic questions, aiming for simplicity and subtlety.

EXERCISE 2 WORKSHEET

Stating Your Purpose
or Mission

Version #1:

_____
_____
_____
_____
_____
_____
_____
_____

Version #2:

_____
_____
_____
_____
_____
_____
_____

Version #3:

_____
_____
_____
_____
_____
_____

Version #4:

_____
_____
_____
_____
_____
_____
_____

Version #5:

_____
_____
_____
_____
_____
_____
_____
_____
_____

STEP B

DETERMINE LEVEL OF COMMITMENT

Once you have stated your company's mission, you will want to make sure everyone in the company understands it and is committed to it. Unless they understand it, people won't embrace it. Given the subtlety of a good mission statement, you must take steps to draw out its implications in detail. When your people discuss it, they should be able to explore its ramifications, tracking and evaluating all the ways in which it can influence the ways they do their jobs, the levels of performance they achieve, and the influences their achievements will have on customers, competitors, and every member of the organization. To increase understanding, you must be extremely patient, taking time to discuss your organization's vision with both individuals and groups.

If your company has not articulated and communicated its purpose before, understanding will take even longer because you will have to replace a multiplicity of previously divergent observations and experiences. In a missionless environment, every employee usually interprets the company's purpose differently, and even the slightest inconsistency with the newly stated mission can lead to misunderstanding.

If you have changed your purpose in any way, you must also allow sufficient time for people to understand the changes. Even small adjustments, no matter how positive, can seem like threats at the outset. A shift in emphasis or mission implies a shift in culture, and a new cultural direction demands even more time, energy, and vigilance than a new strategic direction. If you developed a mission statement years ago, you must regularly reaffirm it. Some people forget the statement, others veer off in

new directions, and new people constantly come aboard. Have you established a formal mechanism for getting the message across to new employees? Do you invest sufficient personal time to increase their understanding?

No matter what your own situation with respect to a mission, remember that different groups within the company will often perceive a mission differently and express varying levels of understanding. If you feel confident that your organization enjoys a high current level of understanding, you must institute a program for attaining and retaining a 100 percent understanding. Impossible? To be sure, not everyone in the organization will understand your purpose to the same degree, but everyone can grasp its essence. If not, that person may not suit your culture and could even pose a threat to it. Screen new people well (we'll talk more about this in Chapter 6 on consistency) and periodically test understanding, but also look for cultural mismatching. The mismatched employee would probably be happier and more productive elsewhere.

After you have articulated your company's purpose and assessed the level of understanding, you can address the problem of getting people to embrace it fully. Only when your people take your vision as their own can commitment begin to build its full momentum. Of course, this sort of "buy-in" greatly depends on the level of understanding. During discussions with individuals and groups concerning their levels of understanding, be alert for comments that indicate people do not accept or will not dedicate their best efforts to the common purpose.

Individual and group commitment also depends on the degree to which people believe their efforts to promote it will satisfy their own needs (security, belonging, recognition, quality of work, and self-actualization). Once they are assured of the benefits, their collective commitment will help them achieve both individual and company goals and, as a result, reach new heights of productivity and profitability. Some executives make the mistake of dealing only with the basic needs—security and belonging—whereas achieving full commitment requires addressing *all* vital needs. In this age of heightened social awareness and consumer concerns, most people want to feel their work benefits not only their personal needs but those of society at large. Satisfying the full range of personal, group, and social needs requires your genuine concern and attention.

You can use a variety of programs to stimulate commitment. Some companies hold focus-group discussions, often involving top management and employees. Others print internal brochures that reaffirm the ways in which the mission will satisfy the full range of needs, and still others rely on slogans that deliver the message to everyone inside and outside the company.

EXERCISE 3
SURVEYING YOUR PEOPLE'S UNDERSTANDING OF THE MISSION

Three basic actions can instill high levels of understanding:

1. Articulate the company's purpose in a simple philosophy or mission statement.
2. Talk about the purpose constantly. Discuss it, explain it, defend it, debate it, present it, write it, and sell it.
3. Tie all strategic and tactical plans and actions to the company's purpose.

Whether you are now performing the three basic actions or not, you should assess the current level of understanding of your company's purpose among your people by regularly surveying selected employees to find out how accurately they can describe the mission. Include top management, a sampling of middle management, and representatives from the general work force. Your surveys can include formal printed questionnaires, informal conversations, informal discussion or focus groups, or formal mission-reevaluation meetings.

You might initiate your survey program by convening top management and asking them to write one paragraph summarizing the company's purpose. Collect and evaluate these paragraphs, then ask the executives to perform the same exercise with the managers who report directly to them. These managers can, in turn, collect paragraphs from their subordinates. And sales or public relations people can seek them from customers and competitors. One executive even put the board of directors and prominent stockholders through this exercise.

When JCN surveyed its people, it found strong understanding among the top management group but a wide divergence of views at the next level of management, which included research scientists and engineers. Once the paragraphs had been collected from the top management group they were consolidated into one statement that corresponded very closely with the purpose statement identified in Exercise 2. When the research scientists were surveyed, their paragraphs, when consolidated, demonstrated a much narrower view of the company's purpose and a lack of customer and profitability awareness.

EXERCISE 3 EXAMPLE

Group 1/*Top Management*
Number of Views: 8% of the Whole: *100*
Consolidated Statement: *To develop the most technically superior hardware and software, and to deliver those products in an informed fashion, thus enabling our customers to advance their own products and our people to enjoy both satisfaction and the benefits of increased profits.*
Notable Exceptions: *None*

Group 2/*Research Scientists*
Number of Views: 22% of the Whole: *100*
Consolidated Statement: *To obtain patents for technical advancements and engineer high-performance products.*
Notable Exceptions: *Lack of customer and profitability awareness.*

Notice how top management's views closely paralleled the original mission statement but the views of the research scientists did not include two key elements. From these results, JCN's CEO determined that he needed to spend more time raising the level of understanding of the research group, on whose efforts the whole company's future would be riding.

Decide beforehand which groups within your company you wish to survey. Some suggestions might include: top management, middle management, rank-and-file employees; or the marketing department, production department, sales force, R&D department; or board of directors, stockholders, customer groups. You can isolate any group of employees in the company to assess their view and understanding of the company's purpose. You may want to divide your company's organization into numerous groups, or keep it to fewer, larger groups—or you may want to try both.

EXERCISE 3 WORKSHEET

Surveying Your People's Understanding of the Mission

Group 1/ _____
Number of Views: _____ **% of the Whole:** _____
Consolidated Statement: _____
_____
_____
_____

Notable Exceptions: _____
_____
_____
_____

Group 2/ _____
Number of Views: _____ **% of the Whole:** _____
Consolidated Statement: _____
_____
_____
_____

Notable Exceptions: _____
_____
_____
_____

Group 3/ _____
Number of Views: _____ **% of the Whole:** _____
Consolidated Statement: _____
_____
_____
_____

Notable Exceptions: _____
_____
_____
_____

Group 4/ _____
Number of Views: _____ **% of the Whole:** _____
Consolidated Statement: _____
_____
_____
_____

Notable Exceptions: _____
_____
_____
_____

Group 5/ _____
Number of Views: _____ **% of the Whole:** _____
Consolidated Statement: _____
_____
_____
_____

Notable Exceptions: _____
_____
_____
_____

Group 6/ _____
Number of Views: _____ **% of the Whole:** _____
Consolidated Statement: _____
_____
_____
_____

Notable Exceptions: _____
_____
_____
_____

EXERCISE 4
PINPOINTING THE CAUSES OF EXCEPTIONS

If you have detected any notable exceptions to a consensus understanding of your mission, you will want to explore what caused the deviations. Almost every thorough survey will uncover some divergence of views, but if yours hasn't, don't sit back and relax, because the next survey one or two years from now probably will.

Returning to JCN, its CEO explored the causes for the lack of complete understanding among the company's research scientists.

EXERCISE 4 EXAMPLE

Group 2/Research Scientists
What caused the exception(s) in Group 2?
- A. *By motivating and rewarding this group for its innovations and patents without properly tying the motivation and rewards to satisfying customer needs, we have reinforced "pure research" over "applications."*
- B. *The group functions as a scientific elite and lacks sufficiently formal ties to the sales and service departments.*
- C. *Research scientists, by their very nature, pursue lines of inquiry for the satisfaction of curiosity more than for a desire to see their breakthroughs result in useful products. They often disdain business and profit goals.*
- D. *Their personalities and hectic schedules have allowed them to be excused from many general meetings and activities.*

Pinpointing the Causes of Exceptions

Group 1/ _____
What caused the exception(s) within Group 1?

    A. _____
_____
_____
_____

    B. _____
_____
_____
_____

    C. _____
_____
_____
_____

    D. _____
_____
_____
_____

Group 2/ _____
What caused the exception(s) within Group 2?

    A. _____
_____
_____
_____

    B. _____
_____
_____
_____

    C. _____
_____
_____
_____

    D. _____
_____
_____
_____

Group 3/ _____
What caused the exception(s) within Group 3?

    A. _____
_____
_____
_____

    B. _____
_____
_____
_____

    C. _____
_____
_____
_____

    D. _____
_____
_____
_____

Group 4/ _____
What caused the exception(s) within Group 4?

    A. _____
_____
_____
_____

    B. _____
_____
_____
_____

    C. _____
_____
_____
_____

    D. _____
_____
_____
_____

Group 5/ _____
What caused the exception(s) within Group 5?

    A. _____
_____
_____
_____

    B. _____
_____
_____
_____

    C. _____
_____
_____
_____

    D. _____
_____
_____
_____

EXERCISE 5
MEASURING LEVELS OF COMMITMENT

Since complete understanding does not necessarily lead people to total commitment to a mission, you must separately weigh levels of commitment. Total commitment depends on two important "buy-in factors":

- Amount of complete understanding of the company's purpose
- Degree to which commitment to company's purpose satisfies individual needs

In this exercise you will assess these factors by rating each one High, Medium, or Low. The first factor's rating will derive from the results of Exercises 3 and 4. Despite the subjective nature of such a judgment, you should try to base your rating on collected facts.

You will find it harder to rate the degree to which commitment to the mission meets individual needs. Try to make your evaluation as objective as possible by not imposing *your* needs on others but striving instead to gauge how well commitment serves the needs of people whose values and ambitions may differ from your own. Carefully consider five basic needs: security (physical well-being, working conditions, compensation, benefits); belonging (social interaction, group dynamics, participation in decision making); recognition (praise, promotions, bonuses, awards); quality of work (work that is interesting, challenging, inspiring, and engaging); and self-actualization (the dreams and desires of your people). The composite of all five categories will form your overall rating. If you decide you lack sufficient data on which to base your ratings, you can again conduct a formal internal survey, but don't wait for the results before trying this exercise.

Finally, based upon the two previous factors, you will rate each management and employee group's current level of commitment to your company's purpose.

As JCN completed this exercise, its executive committee arrived at the following ratings for the research group.

EXERCISE 5 EXAMPLE

Group 2/*Research Scientists*
1. **Amount of complete understanding of the company's purpose?** *Low*
2. **Degree to which commitment to company's purpose satisfies individual needs?** *Overall Rating: Medium*
3. **Current level of commitment?** *Low +*

EXERCISE 5 WORKSHEET

Measuring Levels of Commitment

Group 1/ _____

1. Amount of complete understanding of company purpose?

	High	Medium	Low

2. Degree to which commitment to company's purpose satisfies individual needs?

	High	Medium	Low
Security:	High	Medium	Low
Belonging:	High	Medium	Low
Recognition:	High	Medium	Low
Quality of work:	High	Medium	Low
Self-actualization:	High	Medium	Low
Overall rating:	High	Medium	Low

3. Current level of commitment to company's purpose?

	High	Medium	Low

Group 2/ _____

1. Amount of complete understanding of company purpose?

	High	Medium	Low

2. Degree to which commitment to company's purpose satisfies individual needs?

	High	Medium	Low
Security:	High	Medium	Low
Belonging:	High	Medium	Low
Recognition:	High	Medium	Low
Quality of work:	High	Medium	Low
Self-actualization:	High	Medium	Low
Overall rating:	High	Medium	Low

3. Current level of commitment to company's purpose?

	High	Medium	Low

Group 3/ _____

1. Amount of complete understanding of company purpose?

	High	Medium	Low

2. Degree to which commitment to company's purpose satisfies individual needs?

	High	Medium	Low
Security:	High	Medium	Low
Belonging:	High	Medium	Low
Recognition:	High	Medium	Low
Quality of work:	High	Medium	Low
Self-actualization:	High	Medium	Low
Overall rating:	High	Medium	Low

3. Current level of commitment to company's purpose?

	High	Medium	Low

EXERCISE 5 WORKSHEET (*Cont.*)

Group 4/ _____

1. Amount of complete understanding of company purpose?

	High	Medium	Low

2. Degree to which commitment to company's purpose satisfies individual needs?

	High	Medium	Low
Security:	High	Medium	Low
Belonging:	High	Medium	Low
Recognition:	High	Medium	Low
Quality of work:	High	Medium	Low
Self-actualization:	High	Medium	Low
Overall rating:	High	Medium	Low

3. Current level of commitment to company's purpose?

	High	Medium	Low

Group 5/ _____

1. Amount of complete understanding of company purpose?

	High	Medium	Low

2. Degree to which commitment to company's purpose satisfies individual needs?

	High	Medium	Low
Security:	High	Medium	Low
Belonging:	High	Medium	Low
Recognition:	High	Medium	Low
Quality of work:	High	Medium	Low
Self-actualization:	High	Medium	Low
Overall rating:	High	Medium	Low

3. Current level of commitment to company's purpose?

	High	Medium	Low

Overall Rating of each factor for the company as a whole:

	High	Medium	Low
1.	High	Medium	Low
2.	High	Medium	Low
3.	High	Medium	Low

STEP C

ASSESS THE DEGREE TO WHICH COMMITMENT CREATES EXCELLENCE

Now that you have determined the level of commitment to your company's purpose, you can assess the positive or negative results of that commitment. Positive results depend upon a clear articulation of your company's purpose, a grass-roots understanding of it, and a widespread commitment to it. In order to achieve superior results you must first measure the results currently being achieved and by which groups. Assessing these results requires comparison of the differences between groups that do understand and feel committed to the purpose and those groups that do not.

You will also need to predict the additional results and benefits that could be gained by different groups if they increased their commitment. Can you estimate the added benefits of higher levels of commitment for each group inside the company?

EXERCISE 6
EVALUATING THE RESULTS OF COMMITMENT

For each of the groups identified and analyzed in Exercises 4 and 5, describe the results achieved by each group currently and then project expected results if commitment rose to its highest level. You can describe the results for a group of management or employees in any way that makes sense for your particular business. Results could be described in terms of profit, cost control, sales volume, repeat business, customer satisfaction, productivity measures, downtime, product rejects, or product innovations. We suggest you be as specific as possible in describing results, as JCN was.

EXERCISE 6 EXAMPLE

Group 2/*Research Scientists*

1. **Describe current results:**
   Too much time and money spent on research that never benefits customers or our company. Last year we spent $11 million on research that produced no tangible value. We recognize the need for a "free" research environment, but $11 million is too much when only $3 million translated into new products or product improvements.
2. **Describe expected results when commitment is at highest level:**
   We would expect to spend even more on research than we now do, but the proportion of nontangible value would decline. Last year, for example, we would have ideally spent $11 million on research that got results and $3 million on research that did not.

As you complete this exercise be extremely specific. Your estimate of the expected results when commitment reaches its highest level will provide you with some interesting insights into the value of commitment and into the future improvement your company can expect.

Evaluating the Results of Commitment

Group 1/ _____

1. Describe current results: _____
_____
_____

2. Describe expected results when commitment is
   at highest level: _____
_____
_____

Group 2/ _____

1. Describe current results: _____
_____
_____

2. Describe expected results when commitment is
   at highest level: _____
_____
_____

Group 3/ _____

1. Describe current results: _____
_____
_____

2. Describe expected results when commitment is
   at highest level: _____
_____
_____

Group 4/ _____

1. Describe current results: _____
_____
_____

2. Describe expected results when commitment is
   at highest level: _____
_____
_____

Group 5/ _____

1. Describe current results: _____
_____
_____

2. Describe expected results when commitment is
   at highest level: _____
_____
_____

SUMMARY

You should now record conclusions drawn from this chapter's exercises. Before you begin, consider these examples of JCN's conclusions.

SUMMARY EXAMPLE

PART A

Conclusions from Step A, Exercises 1 and 2

In the past, many of our scientists and engineers have innovated just for innovation's sake rather than with customer needs in mind. For them our mission statement can provide a needed focus for their efforts.

PART B

Conclusions from Step B, Exercises 3, 4, and 5

Our scientists express satisfaction with the freedom we have given them. While we want to get them more fully involved in our mission, we do not want to do so in a way that would damage the current level of satisfaction with their work.

PART C

Conclusions from Step C, Exercise 6

Many of our customers and our own people (especially those in sales and service) perceive our scientists as valuable and skilled but at the same time aloof and out of touch with the real world.

PART D

Overall Summary of Conclusions

We have neglected the need to bring our research scientists into our mission, despite the fact that their work will make or break our strategy. We should take immediate steps to correct this.

PART E

Future Directions

Perhaps we could develop educational programs for our scientists that will help them see the connections between their R&D efforts, satisfied customers, and profitability. Should we put a sales/service representative in their group? Get our scientists out into the field to see their products at work? Invite customers to tour our research facility and have lunch with our scientists? Spend more personal time away from the office with key researchers?

Boil your conclusions down to a few overall insights based on the results of all the exercises in this chapter. These overall conclusions will form one-third of your culture audit, which, combined with the other two-thirds (competence and consistency), you will unite in Chapter 7 with your strategy assessment.

SUMMARY WORKSHEET

PART A

Conclusions from Step A, Exercises 1 and 2, pages 83—85

1. _____
_____
_____
_____
_____

2. _____
_____
_____
_____

3. _____
_____
_____
_____

PART B

Conclusions from Step B, Exercises 3, 4, and 5, pages 89—94

1. _____
_____
_____
_____

2. _____
_____
_____
_____

3. _____
_____
_____
_____

PART C

Conclusions from Step C, Exercise 6, page 96

1. _____
_____
_____
_____

2. _____
_____
_____

3. _____
_____
_____
_____

PART D

Overall Summary of Conclusions

1. _____
_____
_____
_____

2. _____
_____
_____

3. _____
_____
_____

4. _____
_____
_____

5. _____
_____
_____
_____
_____
_____

6. _____
_____
_____
_____
_____
_____

PART E
Future Directions

_____
_____
_____
_____
_____
_____
_____
_____
_____
_____
_____
_____
_____
_____
_____
_____

Strong cultures depend on high levels of commitment to a common purpose, without which no organization can create long-range excellence. But commitment alone cannot build a strong culture; it must combine with organization-wide competence to deliver superior performance, a topic we'll take up in the next chapter.

5

DEVELOPING COMPETENCE TO DELIVER SUPERIOR PERFORMANCE

Most of us recognize what highly visible, successful companies do well. IBM provides unsurpassed customer service, General Electric strategically manages its businesses better than any other conglomerate, and Coke and Pepsi display remarkable marketing skill. The competencies of these and other well-known companies lie at the very heart of their excellence.

By competence we mean an organization's dominant skill or capability, the activity or function or process the organization has perfected over all others and that it uses to satisfy customers and dominate competitors. Don't confuse competence and strength. A company may enjoy numerous strengths that do not necessarily result in competence. Coke and Pepsi, for example, continue to apply their marketing competence to control over 60 percent of the soft-drink industry, increasing their combined market shares in 1984 from 64.7 percent to 66.3 percent, an increase of $420 million. However, while Coca-Cola, ranked by *Fortune*'s 1985 survey as the second most admired company in America (behind IBM), has numerous resources and abilities that translate into company strengths, these strengths do not represent the company's *overriding* competence or *dominant* skill. To be sure, Coke combines its distribution network resource with skillful management of independent bottlers to produce distribution prowess; it combines its financial asset resources with cost and asset management abilities to produce a great strength in asset utilization; and it combines its customer loyalty resource with its own innovation ability to produce successful new products, such as diet Coke. Although such strengths play a vital role in the company's success, Coke's overriding competence is marketing. From getting more shelf space in stores to developing award-winning national advertising campaigns, Coke does it all extremely well despite the recent controversy surrounding the introduction of "New Coke" and the introduction of "Classic Coke."

In fact, you can easily pinpoint any company's overriding competence by answering one key question: "What does it do *extremely* well?" The answer will penetrate to the very core of an organization's culture, because everyone in the company participates in that competence. Coca-Cola's executives hope that even an employee involved in producing syrup at Coke will take pride in the fact that the results of his or her efforts will be aggressively marketed around the world. We strongly believe that companies with one overriding, dominant skill achieve excellence because that skill augments the cohesiveness and sense of unity that make it unbeatable in the marketplace. Without such a dominant competence, no company can build the strong culture it needs to create excellence.

Astrotech International Corporation, reporting an $8 million loss in the first quarter of fiscal 1985, ran afoul of the rule of competence in its Special Metals Corporation subsidiary, a manufacturer of superalloys for the aerospace industry. In that business, metals must be flawless and meet excruciatingly exact specifications. If an alloy fails to meet the specs, you end up writing it off. Unfortunately, Special Metals lacked sufficient competence in this area, and Astrotech's chairman Willard Rockwell had to publicly admit "unusual production problems" to *The Wall Street Journal*. Put another way, Special Metals failed to develop the overriding competence upon which its success depended.

By contrast Merck, the pharmaceutical giant, has stressed competence in research, the one area on which the company could rely for lasting success. Since scientists tend to value the freedom to pursue intriguing lines of research, Merck attracts the best scientists by offering an unusual degree of freedom. The company's unrelenting commitment in this area has not only helped propel it to the top of the nation's drug industry, but has also produced some rather remarkable, unexpected benefits. Many years ago Merck scientists were conducting research on Addison's disease, a disease that affects such a relatively small number of people that most pharmaceutical companies would have shunned it. Merck's research eventually resulted in the discovery of cortisone, a revolutionary drug to combat arthritis. If Merck had prohibited the Addison's disease research, it would not have stumbled upon cortisone, and the company would not have won its leadership position in the industry.

Cortisone was not a fluke. Merck spends 11 percent of sales on research, compared to an industry average of only 6.7 percent. In 1985 alone Merck allocated $400 million to this area of competence, and its chairman, John Horan, constantly emphasizes its long-range benefits. At a time when most competitors abandoned vaccines in light of low profitability and potential liability, Merck forged ahead with a new hepatitis vaccine that now generates healthy profits. Roy Vagelos, executive vice president in charge of Merck's research effort and Horan's heir apparent, encourages his people to pursue all medical leads. When the researchers came up with a breakthrough drug for river blindness, an African disease causing loss of eyesight, Merck immediately tested the drug in Africa, despite unfavorable projected financial returns. A spin-off from the river-blindness research produced a worming agent for horses that will strongly enhance the company's animal products line. Merck's success springs from an overriding and unifying competence that has brought an average 22 percent return on equity over the past five years. It is small wonder that *Fortune* ranks the $3.2 billion company as one of the ten most admired companies in America.

To develop and maintain your own company's overriding competence you must take three important steps:

Step A: *Analyze historical competencies*
Step B: *Determine dominant competence*
Step C: *Gauge performance*

As with previous exercises, you will carefully analyze your past accomplishments before you zero in on your current position. Though you will once again be brainstorming for insights into how you might improve your position, remember that at this point your efforts should concentrate on assessment, not action.

STEP A

ANALYZE HISTORICAL COMPETENCIES

Does an overriding, collectively shared skill or capability rest at the core of your company? Before answering this question, you should break your corporate history into distinct "eras," examining key events, decisions, and results of each era in turn. Only then can you begin to identify the overriding competence of each era. Perhaps you will find that your company's competence has evolved from era to era, or you may discover dramatic changes or even the erosion or disappearance of a dominant competence in a given era. As we saw with Merck, a successful company matches its overriding competence to the critical success factors in its industry. Any matches and mismatches you uncover from era to era reveal important clues about how you can turn your company's past and present into a brighter future.

To gain further insight into historical competence you should evaluate how people in your organization "made it" in the past. How has "making it" or "climbing the corporate ladder" changed from era to era? Understanding the reasons why people have succeeded and failed in your company will provide added insight into the nature of the company's historically dominant competence.

EXERCISE 1

IDENTIFYING ERAS AND CRITICAL SUCCESS FACTORS

Taking advantage of insights into your company's competence depends on identifying the distinct historical eras your company has experienced. By eras we mean blocks of time set apart by certain boundaries. These boundaries vary from company to company. Some use size as a boundary ("In 1967 we were small, in 1977 we were medium-sized, in 1985 we were large"). Others, especially those in volatile industries, may use shifts in consumer tastes, in competition, or in the types of products or services offered, while still others may use the succession of new management teams. Apple Computer might adopt the size boundaries (pre- and post-Macintosh), Delta Airlines might compartmentalize pre- and post-deregulation, and ITT might employ the stepping down of Harold Geneen, which marked the end of an era of acquisition and growth.

Whether controlled by external or internal factors, an era may last from a few to many years, but each era brings with it a specific set of critical success factors. In every business the factors that determine success constantly change as the business environment evolves, and major evolutionary epochs in that environment provide the most striking clues to historical competencies. Critical success factors may vary slightly or dramatically from era to era. Can Apple's upstart culture operate a mature enterprise? Can Delta Airlines change from pre-deregulation goals of maximizing the number of once-profitable long-haul flights to post-deregulation goals of maximizing the now-profitable short-haul flights? Can ITT add technology management to its superior financial management?

Exercise 1 will help you identify eras and their corresponding success factors. Before you complete it for your own company, observe how a Midwestern electric utility company approached this task. Soon after the turn of the century, Midwest Power (MWP) emerged from among a number of independent companies to become one of the leading utilities in the region. A "family" atmosphere permeated MWP both internally and externally as it focused on providing affordable electricity to all its customers. During the depression of the 1930s it did not lay off its people but reduced expenses by reducing wages. This tradition continued until well after World War II as the region MWP served enjoyed prosperous growth. Before the war the utility had relied on hydroelectric power generation, but the expansion of residential and industrial customers forced it into thermal generation, where technological advances made coal-fired generating stations attractive. MWP's competence in constructing such facilities resulted in relatively low new-plant costs and, as a consequence, only infrequent rate increases. During this era the utility enjoyed a booming economy, increasing electricity demand, stable costs, a highly favorable competitive advantage, and widespread customer and community support.

However, in the early 1970s environmental awareness among consumers prompted new government regulation, and the 1973–74 oil embargo crisis and recession caused costs of utility equipment and operations to skyrocket. MWP nevertheless continued to grow during this period, constructing major new generating plants. The cost of this expansion required sharp increases in revenues. As rate increases became more frequent, customers grew increasingly unhappy over their utility bills. Feeling pressure from all sides, MWP's new CEO launched a strategic planning process that included an evaluation of his organization's historically dominant competence. As he and his executive team undertook Exercise 1, they identified five distinct eras and their critical success factors:

EXERCISE 1 EXAMPLE

Era	Salient Feature	Critical Success Factors
1895–1910	*Independent suppliers*	1. *Effective coordination with other electricity suppliers* 2. *Successful mergers with other electricity suppliers*
1911–1944	*Community welfare*	1. *Making electricity available* 2. *Ensuring the reliability of electricity*
1945–1972	*Rapid growth*	1. *Successful power plant construction* 2. *Expansion of distribution systems*
1973–1985	*Cost consciousness*	1. *Controlling costs of supplying electricity* 2. *Getting rate increases*
1985–	*Customer responsiveness*	1. *Providing customers with energy alternatives* 2. *Participating in technological advances*

Before you begin Exercise 1, you will want to collect as much of your corporate history as possible. Retired managers and employees, informal company historians (from the retired personnel director who has seen it all to the secretary celebrating her fiftieth anniversary with the firm), and archives containing published articles and interviews can all supply valuable data. Even if your company has not yet reached its fifth birthday, you will profit from sitting back to view its history. Out of your history will spring your future.

Identifying Eras and Critical Success Factors

Era	Salient Feature	Critical Success Factors
_____	_____	1. _____
	_____	_____
		_____
		_____
		2. _____
		_____
		_____
		3. _____
		_____
		_____
		_____
_____	_____	1. _____
	_____	_____
		_____
		2. _____
		_____
		_____
		3. _____
		_____
		_____
		_____
_____	_____	1. _____
	_____	_____
		_____
		2. _____
		_____
		3. _____
		_____
		_____
		_____

_____   _____   1. _____
                    _____   _____
                                               _____
                                            2. _____
                                               _____
                                               _____
                                            3. _____
                                               _____
                                               _____

_____   _____   1. _____
                    _____   _____
                                               _____
                                            2. _____
                                               _____
                                               _____
                                            3. _____
                                               _____
                                               _____

Future Era

_____   _____   1. _____
                    _____   _____
                                            2. _____
                                               _____
                                            3. _____
                                               _____
                                               _____

EXERCISE 2
EVALUATING ERAS AND COMPANY COMPETENCE

In this exercise you will describe your company's competence during each of its eras. Consider to what degree people displayed competence at controlling or addressing the critical success factors. Was there a close correlation between competencies and success factors? To determine matches and mismatches, list the major events, decisions, and key people during each era. Why were they noteworthy? Look for events that offered threats as well as opportunities, bad as well as good decisions, successful and unsuccessful people—because all these elements will help explain an era's competence.

MWP's senior executives determined that the company's overriding competence in the most recent era was "defending its position." As they evaluated the major events, decisions, and people of the last decade, they realized that most elements related to justifying the company's rate increases, resolving public service commission inquiries, dealing with adverse publicity, and soothing irate customers. During the same era, the critical success factors were: controlling the cost of electricity, obtaining rate increases, and turning the tide of public opinion—a strong correlation with the competence displayed during the era. Bear in mind that MWP performed the summary below for *each* of its eras.

EXERCISE 2 EXAMPLE

Era: *Cost Consciousness (1973–1985)*

Major events, decisions, or people:

The numerous rate cases over the last several years were always major events because they affected every department in the company. Every department had to prepare information for the rate cases and then had to implement new rates with customers. The most important decisions over this period were the two decisions to build new power plants because those plants cost several hundred million dollars each and required several increases in rates. We have consistently motivated and rewarded our people, especially the lawyers and the financial executives who paved the way for rate increases with the commission.

How major events, decisions, and people shaped competence:

Given our preoccupation with rate cases and favorable treatment by regulatory bodies, state and municipal governments, and the public at large, the company built on its long-standing competence of effectively managing outside relationships to develop a genuine expertise in defending its position, whether a rate increase, a new plant, a new rate schedule for a particular class of customer, or a required return on investment for stockholders. The events and decisions dealt with the survival of the company in an increasingly hostile world, and the most influential people in the company were those who could respond most quickly during times of crisis.

Overriding company competence:

Defending our position. By this we mean the ability to successfully defend the company against customer and public outcries, to succeed in requesting and getting needed rate increases, and to maintain an adequate return on investment.

As you complete Exercise 2, be wary of superficial descriptions of competence. Before the utility executives wrote "defending our position," they discarded a number of statements that only partially explained the company's competence during the recent era: "getting rate increases," "political maneuvering," "quick reaction to threats," and "keeping critics at bay." Again, put some creative thought into the final part of the exercise, Future Era.

EXERCISE 2 WORKSHEET

Evaluating Eras and Company Competence

Era: _____
Major events, decisions, or people: _____

_____
_____
_____
_____
_____
_____
_____
_____
_____
_____
_____
_____

How major events, decisions, and people
shaped competence: _____

_____
_____
_____
_____
_____
_____
_____
_____
_____
_____
_____
_____

Overriding company competence: _____

_____
_____
_____
_____
_____
_____
_____
_____

Era: _____
Major events, decisions, or people: _____

_____
_____
_____
_____
_____
_____
_____
_____
_____
_____
_____
_____

How major events, decisions, and people
shaped competence: _____

_____
_____
_____
_____
_____
_____
_____
_____
_____

Overriding company competence: _____

_____
_____
_____
_____
_____
_____
_____
_____
_____

Era: _____
Major events, decisions, or people: _____

_____
_____

EXERCISE 2 WORKSHEET (*Cont.*)

_____

_____

_____

_____

_____

_____

_____

_____

How major events, decisions, and people shaped competence: _____

_____

_____

_____

_____

_____

_____

_____

_____

_____

Overriding company competence: _____

_____

_____

_____

_____

_____

_____

Era: _____
Major events, decisions, or people: _____

_____

_____

_____

_____

_____

_____

_____

_____

_____

_____

How major events, decisions, and people shaped competence: _____

_____

_____

_____

_____

_____

_____

Overriding company competence: _____

_____

_____

_____

_____

_____

_____

Future Era: _____
Major events, decisions, or people: _____

_____

_____

_____

_____

_____

_____
_____
_____
_____
_____

How major events, decisions, and people will shape competence: _____
_____
_____
_____
_____
_____
_____
_____
_____
_____
_____
_____
_____
_____

Overriding company competence: _____
_____
_____
_____
_____
_____
_____
_____

STEP B

DETERMINE DOMINANT COMPETENCE

After you have thoroughly analyzed your company's historical competencies, you can more fully detail the direction of its currently dominant one. Remember, competence is more than a strength, and it must be shared collectively with everyone in the organization. At Merck, for example, salesmen do not conduct scientific research but they do sell research every day, explaining research results, new research projects, a drug's performance, the value of basic research to customers, and the achievements of Merck's scientists. Just as important, Merck salesmen bring back from customers valuable feedback about needs the researchers might explore. Some employees in your own company may contribute more directly to the overriding competence than others, but everyone must recognize and respect that competence.

Keep your historical perspective in mind and review the company strengths you identified in Chapter 3, because your company's competence derives to some extent from some combination of those strengths. Furthermore, competence should arise from your company's commitment to a common purpose (Chapter 4).

DETERMINING YOUR COMPANY'S DOMINANT COMPETENCE

In this exercise you will be detailing your company's current competence. Even though you identified your current era's competence in Exercise 2, here you will be viewing it from another perspective, assessing "manifestations of competence" and the "causes" of those manifestations. When you examine the causes, you will be exposing the fundamental organizational capabilities that have gotten you to where you are now.

Again consider Midwest Power, whose executives identified several manifestations of competence and exposed their company's dominant competence (see facing page).

EXERCISE 3 EXAMPLE

Manifestations of Competence	Causes
1. *Getting every rate increase requested over the last ten years.*	*Effective management of regulatory relationships.*
2. *Initiating seventy-eight bills in three state legislatures to improve and streamline regulation.*	*Effective management of legislative relationships.*
3. *Keeping ten municipal governments from choosing to operate their own utilities.*	*Effective management of political relationships.*
4. *Reducing customer complaints from over 5% to under 1% in a two-year period.*	*Effective management of public (customer) relationships.*

5. Based on the foregoing analysis of manifestations and causes, what is your company's dominant competence? *The effective management of all public, political, legislative and regulatory relationships to successfully defend our position.*

Although the preceding example shows only four of the strongest manifestations of competence, MWP actually identified twenty-six during this exercise. When you complete the exercise for your own company, list every possible recent manifestation of your competence.

Determining Your Company's Dominant Competence

**Manifestations
of Competence**   **Causes**

1. _____   _____
   _____   _____
   _____   _____

2. _____   _____
   _____   _____
   _____   _____

3. _____   _____
   _____   _____
   _____   _____

4. _____   _____
   _____   _____
   _____   _____

5. _____   _____
   _____   _____
   _____   _____

6. _____   _____
   _____   _____
   _____   _____

7. _____   _____
   _____   _____
   _____   _____

8. _____   _____
   _____   _____
   _____   _____

9. _____   _____
   _____   _____
   _____   _____

10. _____   _____
    _____   _____
    _____   _____

11. _____   _____
    _____   _____
    _____   _____

12. _____   _____
    _____   _____
    _____   _____

13. _____   _____
    _____   _____
    _____   _____

14. _____   _____
    _____   _____
    _____   _____

15. _____   _____
    _____   _____
    _____   _____

16. _____   _____
    _____   _____
    _____   _____

17. _____   _____
    _____   _____
    _____   _____

18. _____   _____
    _____   _____
    _____   _____

19. _____   _____
    _____   _____
    _____   _____

20. _____   _____
    _____   _____
    _____   _____

**Based on the foregoing analysis of
manifestations and causes, what is your
company's dominant competence?**

_____
_____
_____

EXERCISE 4
TESTING YOUR COMPETENCE

In this exercise you will test the competence you identified in Exercise 3 to see if it meets the criteria of a successful dominant competence. Just as every strength does not necessarily result in competence, especially if a strength lies dormant or underutilized, neither do all competencies support success. In the case of Midwest Power, for example, the ability to defend the company's position might protect the company's past success, but its continuance might actually stifle long-range success if a new era demands technological innovation and the development of energy alternatives for customers.

Your answers to the ten questions on the following test should help you judge to what extent perpetuation of the competence will help create lasting excellence. If the competence you have identified does not pass this test, you may not want to perpetuate it. The only thing worse than not having a dominant competence is having one you do not fully understand.

When the utility executives completed Exercise 4, they answered yes to every question but the last two, which dealt with the future. In answering no to these questions and yes to the others, they quickly realized that what they had identified as the company's competence was truly a dominant competence, but that it probably wouldn't meet the needs of the future.

EXERCISE 4 WORKSHEET

Testing Your Competence

	Yes	No
1. Does the identified competence follow in a logical way from the company's historical competencies?	____	____
2. Are there numerous (at least ten) manifestations of the dominant competence?	____	____
3. Is there a direct link between the critical success factors for the current era and the identified dominant competence?	____	____
4. Are the company strengths identified in Chapter 4 consistent with and supportive of the identified dominant competence?	____	____
5. Is the identified dominant competence collectively held by a majority of people in the organization such that they directly or indirectly demonstrate the competence?	____	____
6. Are the roots or basis of the identified dominant competence long-standing with this organization?	____	____
7. Do the major events, significant decisions, and influential people of the current era point to the identified dominant competence as the company's overriding competence?	____	____

8. As you ask yourself the question "What are we really good at around here?" does the identified dominant competence readily come to mind? ____ ____

9. Is there a correlation between the critical success factors for the next era (future) and the identified dominant competence? ____ ____

10. Will the identified dominant competence remain in place for an extended period of time (a minimum of five years)? ____ ____

By the end of this exercise you should not only grasp the extent to which your company's dominant competence has ensured success in the past and during the present era, but you should have a growing sense of where continued reliance on this competence will take you in the future.

STEP C

GAUGE PERFORMANCE

Regardless of the degree to which a perpetuation of your company's current competence will support your future success, you must accurately gauge the level of performance your people are achieving. An objective measurement should take into account both absolute and relative levels of performance. What absolute value does your company's competence deliver to customers? Answer this question without comparing your competence with any of your other capabilities or those of your competitors. Once you have evaluated performance in absolute terms, you can then evaluate it in relative terms. How does your performance stack up against competitors? Against other capabilities within your own organization? If your people's performance allows your company to dominate competitors, this competence provides a significant strategic weapon; if it does not, you must search for ways to enhance or modify the competence. The company with a dominant competence identical to everyone else's in the industry will seldom establish a competitive edge or increase profitability and return. In the long run, your success will come from careful coordination between competence, a culture component, and competitive advantage, a strategy component. Some companies conclude that their competence won't produce a long-range competitive advantage and dump the old competence in favor of a brand-new one. Unfortunately, competence, like commitment, comes only after long and careful nurturing.

Once you have assessed performance relative to competitors, you can evaluate how well the competence draws upon the strengths of your company. Sometimes a dominant competence will grow up in response to a significant need in the environment, but as the company continues to develop and build new strengths over time, the dominant competence fails to draw upon new strengths or respond to major changes in the environment. For example, a large accounting firm, whose dominant competence consisted of providing personalized client attention, had developed sophisticated communications and data-processing systems to support its technical accounting services but had never drawn upon this technical expertise to enhance or improve personalized client attention.

After considering how your dominant competence draws upon company strengths, you will rate the performance of your company's dominant competence compared to other companies in related and unrelated industries. Has the dominant competence really delivered superior performance in the past? Does it now? Will it in the future? If not, it will not contribute to the success of your strategy to satisfy customers, win sustainable advantages over competitors, and capitalize on company strengths. In this exercise you will rate the performance of your company's dominant competence in five areas, the first three of which relate to your strategy:

- Value created for customers
- Dominance over competitors
- Exploitation of company strengths
- Comparison to companies in related and unrelated industries
- Comparison to other competencies in your own company

With performance ratings and an overall total score in hand you can answer some crucial questions about perpetuating your competence.

The utility executives were surprised to find their ratings lower than expected, and they soon realized that MWP's dominant competence caused a defensive/reactive stance rather than the positive and active one a business needs to thrive in an era of accelerating change. An organization that waits for crises or threats before taking action may become good at solving problems and surviving from crisis to crisis, but it will not aggressively create a prosperous future. While the reactive competence had served the utility well over the past decade, the executives began thinking about ways to modify that competence and direct its energy toward opportunities and innovations rather than crises.

EVALUATING ABSOLUTE AND RELATIVE PERFORMANCE

MWP filled out the first section of Exercise 5 as on the facing page.

Superior 5	Good 4	Fair 3	Poor 2	Bad 1

1. Rate your company's dominant competence in terms of the value it creates for your customers.

   ___3___

   Reasons for rating:
   a. *The company stays in business.*
   b. *Customers receive electricity.*
   c. *Customer is not the focus.*

2. Rate the performance of your company's dominant competence when compared to your competitors as a group.

   ___5___

   Reasons for rating:
   a. *Long-standing relationships.*
   b. *Sufficient human resources.*
   c. *Competitors lack clout.*

3. Rate your company's dominant competence in terms of how it draws upon or applies company's strengths.

   ___2___

   Reasons for rating:
   a. *Many strengths are underutilized.*
   b. *Competence is reactive, not active.*
   c. *Competence is narrowly applied.*

4. Rate your company's dominant competence when compared to the competence of *other electric utilities in the country.*

   ___5___

   Reasons for rating:
   a. *We are ahead of other utilities.*
   b. *Many cannot get rate increases.*
   c. *Our record is one of the best.*

5. Rate the performance of your company's dominant competence when compared to other competencies inside your company.

   ___5___

   Reasons for rating:
   a. *Recent management audit results.*
   b. *Top management assessment.*
   c. *Consultants' report.*

Total score: ___20___

For scores of 15 to 22, answer this question: What can you do to improve performance?

Our performance is lower than we'd like to see in creating value for our customers and in drawing upon company strengths. Our competence has protected and defended the company but has not helped customers desiring more control over energy costs, and it has not helped the company to take full advantage of its technical expertise. With new focus on customers and company strengths we can use our dominant competence to pave the way for offering our customers more choices in terms of rates, services, and products. And we can also use our dominant competence to find ways to allow the company to enter into related businesses that will exploit many of the company's technical, energy-management-related strengths.

For all scores, answer this question: If you were to score your company again in the next era (future), what would you guess would be the score and why?

Future score: ___15___   *Because customers will become less satisfied and competitors will strive to serve them, reducing our advantage.*

As you weigh your own company's competence in each of the five areas, take care to identify concrete reasons for your ratings.

Evaluating Absolute and Relative Performance

Superior 5	Good 4	Fair 3	Poor 2	Bad 1

1. Rate your company's dominant competence in terms of the value it creates for your customers.

   Reasons for rating:
   a. _____
   b. _____
   c. _____

2. Rate the performance of your company's dominant competence when compared to your competitors as a group.

   Reasons for rating:
   a. _____
   b. _____
   c. _____

3. Rate your company's dominant competence in terms of how it draws upon or applies your company's strengths.

   Reasons for rating:
   a. _____
   b. _____
   c. _____

4. Rate the performance of your company's dominant competence when compared to the competence of _____
   _____

   Reasons for rating:
   a. _____
   b. _____
   c. _____

5. Rate the performance of your company's dominant competence when compared to other competencies inside your company.

   Reasons for rating:
   a. _____
   b. _____
   c. _____

Total score: _____

For scores of 23 to 25, answer this question: What are you doing to maintain the superior performance of your company's dominant competence? _____

_____
_____
_____
_____
_____
_____

For scores of 15 to 22, answer this question: What can you do to improve the performance of your company's dominant competence? _____

_____
_____
_____
_____
_____
_____

For scores of 14 or under, answer this question: Can you find new ways of applying your company's dominant competence, or should you strive to build a new competence? _____

_____
_____
_____
_____
_____
_____

For all scores, answer this question: If you were to score your company again in the next era (future), what would you guess would be the score and why?

Future score: _____   _____
_____
_____
_____
_____
_____
_____
_____
_____
_____

SUMMARY

Now record your conclusions from all five exercises. In the next column is a sampling from Midwest Power's conclusions.

SUMMARY EXAMPLE

PART A

Conclusions from Step A, Exercises 1 and 2

Our competence has changed during each era, in some cases substantially, in other cases slightly.

PART B

Conclusions from Step B, Exercises 3 and 4

Our dominant competence influences everything our people do, from how we react to customer complaints to how we construct power plants (a fact we formerly ignored).

PART C

Conclusions from Step C, Exercise 5

We should consider redirecting our competence to encourage all the public service commissions to allow us to offer more energy alternatives to our customers, and we should reemphasize our historical technical competence by entering energy-related businesses that will permit greater utilization of our technical energy-management strengths.

PART D

Overall Summary of Conclusions

A shift in emphasis from defensive competence to a stronger customer orientation could position our company to use technology and diversification to make our products and services the first choice of customers, thereby sustaining our competitive edge and more fully capitalizing on our strengths.

PART E

Future Directions

Although a new emphasis seems so logical, it will take tremendous time and energy to move our people from a view of the outside world as hostile to a view that our customers' needs come first and foremost. Could focus groups with our customers help our people change their points of view?

SUMMARY WORKSHEET

PART A

Conclusions from Step A, Exercises 1 and 2, pages 104–109

1. _____
_____
_____
_____

2. _____
_____
_____
_____

3. _____
_____
_____
_____

PART B

Conclusions from Step B, Exercises 3 and 4, pages 112–114

1. _____
_____
_____
_____

2. _____
_____
_____
_____

3. _____
_____
_____
_____

PART C

Conclusions from Step C, Exercise 5, pages 118–119

1. _____
_____
_____
_____

2. _____
_____
_____
_____

3. _____
_____
_____
_____

PART D

Overall Summary of Conclusions

1. _____
_____
_____
_____

2. _____
_____
_____
_____

3. _____
_____
_____
_____

4. _____
_____
_____
_____

SUMMARY WORKSHEET (*Cont.*)

5. _____
_____
_____
_____
_____
_____

6. _____
_____
_____
_____
_____
_____

PART E

Future Directions

_____
_____
_____
_____
_____
_____
_____
_____
_____
_____
_____
_____
_____
_____

In the next chapter we'll see how both competence and commitment depend on consistency. Suppose you've concluded that a perpetuation or modification of your dominant competence will spur your organization to unparalleled success in the future. And suppose, further, that you know how to get your people to embrace a full commitment to your purpose. What then?

CHAPTER 6

PERPETUATING COMMITMENT AND COMPETENCE THROUGH CONSISTENCY

Many companies adapt to change by trying to cash in on trends, but they seldom succeed with such opportunistic strategies if doing so causes them to lose sight of their basic cultural traits. A company must adapt to or initiate change with consistency, a fact IBM almost never forgets.

Amid all the change in the fast-paced information technology world, IBM stands as a beacon of consistency. However, even IBM, the most admired of American corporations, has to remind itself to honor its primary consistency of providing superior service to business customers. After launching the PC, its successful personal computer, IBM followed up with an even smaller machine, the PCjr, a consumer-oriented product that IBM could not fully support with its famous service consistency. Although customers bought 275,000 PCjr's in 1984, those buyers were attracted more by slashed prices than by the promise of service. In early 1985 IBM accepted this fact, curtailed production of the machine, and rededicated itself to the perennial consistency

with which it had always dominated the business market. Perhaps IBM should have known it couldn't dominate the home market with service, but, as so often happens, it let its eagerness to capitalize on change override a basic cultural trait.

Book publishing offers a fascinating example of a whole industry overlooking consistency in favor of opportunism. In 1981 many traditional book publishers, including Simon & Schuster, Prentice-Hall, John Wiley & Sons, Avon, and William Morrow, responded to the personal-computer craze by quickly acquiring thousands of titles. They assigned whole teams of editors to the new product lines and spent millions of dollars on advances to authors. But by late 1984 almost all the publishers were slashing their staffs and drastically reducing their lists of new titles. Simon & Schuster bought more cautiously and lost its key editor in charge of the computer books division; Prentice-Hall cut its future list from 1,500 to 350; John Wiley suffered losses and curtailed its budding software division; Avon dropped plans to build its list; and William Morrow decided not to review new computer-related manuscripts.

Obviously, publishers were caught by surprise when the much-heralded microcomputer revolution fizzled, but the reason for the shock was the fact that, in their opportunistic haste to exploit what promised to be a megatrend, they forgot to consistently apply some of the time-honored values in publishing that had served them so well. Almost everyone made the same basic mistakes: publishers signed up books that would compete with a dozen products from other houses, paid less attention to quality of individual manuscripts, and did not carefully consider the long-term prospects in the field.

In sharp contrast, Tupperware did not make a mistake when it had to respond to new trends. Not long ago Tupperware, famous for its direct-sales "Tupperware parties," found itself in trouble as its once-invincible program deteriorated in the face of problems posed by the increasing numbers of working women, the growing sophistication of homemakers, the availability of cheaper plastic containers in retail outlets, and the saturation of the market with Tupperware "demonstrations." As a result, fewer women attended Tupperware parties, and in

1984 the company's sales fell 6 percent and earnings fell 27 percent. In fact, a three-year slide in earnings and sales at Tupperware caused it to drop from a 28 percent contribution to parent company Dart & Kraft's operating earnings in 1980 to only 14 percent in 1984. Attempting to reverse the trend, the company has shifted its emphasis from "getting more dealers" to "highlighting products" in its advertising, and it has announced a new product line called Ultra 21, a set of plastic cookware designed for use in the freezer, microwave, and the conventional oven.

Although Tupperware knew it had to initiate such changes to survive, it was smart enough not to change a vital aspect of its culture—the direct-sales party program. Changes in the marketplace demanded a more flexible program, with shorter, less formal parties that prospective buyers could attend during office lunch breaks and in health clubs. The company nevertheless adhered to a long-standing consistency by maintaining the essence of its direct-sales approach. After all, Tupperware's ability to inspire commitment among its dealers, who in turn developed remarkable competence at selling products at parties, had made the company famous. To toss all that away would have destroyed a valuable cultural trait. To their credit, Tupperware chairman Douglas Martin and president William Jackson understood their corporate culture well enough not to throw the baby out with the bathwater.

Perpetuating commitment and competence through consistency provides the third ingredient of a strong, healthy corporate culture. To instill consistency in their organizations, execupreneurs pay attention to both their people and their business processes. Beyond simply attracting, developing, rewarding, promoting, and keeping the sort of people who will commit their best efforts to the company mission, the execupreneur must also establish management and operating processes that will direct those efforts in the right direction. Without consistency with respect to people and processes, a company will eventually slide into the ranks of the mediocre.

To make sure you respond to or initiate changes consistently, you should take three fundamental steps:

Step A: *Find consistencies in your company*

Step B: *Judge the positive and negative effects of consistencies*

Step C: *Determine whether your consistencies can perpetuate commitment and competence*

Not all consistencies lead to excellence; some consistencies are merely bad habits or symptoms of inertia. You must learn to tell the difference.

STEP A

FIND CONSISTENCIES IN YOUR COMPANY

First you must identify consistencies in your people and processes. Most parents would agree that successful child-rearing depends less on strictness than on the consistency with which they reward or punish their children for following whatever rules have been laid down. If a child knows its parents expect obedience to a given rule in all similar situations (such as "Don't ever play in the street"), the child will seldom feel confused when it encounters a different situation (for example, where neighborhood kids are allowed to play in a certain street).

Without implying that executives should treat their employees paternalistically, we do suggest that people in organizations need simple, general consistencies to help them avoid wasting time trying to figure out what to do when a new situation or problem arises; and they certainly need the benefit of the consistent examples of their leaders.

In what ways have you motivated and rewarded people over the past five years? Have decision-making processes remained unchanged in a given era or perhaps throughout all eras? These and similar questions will get you started thinking about your company's consistencies. Once you have made such thinking a habit, you can direct it toward a more detailed examination of people and processes. How consistently has your company screened, hired, trained, motivated, rewarded, promoted, disciplined, and terminated employees? How consistently have your managers adhered to the processes by which they analyze, plan, decide, communicate, control, and measure performance?

EXERCISE 1
IDENTIFYING CONSISTENCIES IN PEOPLE PRACTICES

This first exercise will help you detail the consistencies with which your company handles its people, but before you begin, consider the M&M Distribution Corporation, a large, almost $1-billion-a-year company that ships everything from pharmaceuticals and cosmetics to toys and clothing to drug, variety, discount, specialty, and grocery stores throughout the country. M&M buys high volumes of products from manufacturers, and it attracts customers who prefer one-stop buying to the hassles of dealing directly with many suppliers. M&M warehouses all its products and stocks the shelves of stores as necessary. Even though stores pay a little more for M&M's services, they save a great deal of time and paperwork.

To achieve its current size, M&M acquired fifteen different distribution companies over the last three years. These new companies accounted for over half of M&M's sales, the other half coming from M&M's own thirty-year-old Marshal & Myers Distributing. Such a conglomeration of acquisitions has made consistency a top priority for the company. As M&M's CEO completed Exercise 1, he found only two major consistencies relating to people practices: the compensation of salespeople and the training of new salespeople. Here's how he completed questions 3 and 6.

EXERCISE 1 EXAMPLE

People Practices	Description of Consistencies
3. Indoctrinating new recruits	*Every new salesperson we hire goes through an intensive six-month indoctrination and training program during which he or she spends time working in the warehouse, accompanying*

125

	an experienced salesperson, and taking customer service calls. We've been doing this for five years with each salesperson in each company we've acquired.
6. Rewarding employees	*Ten years ago we developed a compensation system combining salary and commission that has set the standard for our industry. Competitors copy it but no one administers it as well as we do.*

As you tackle Exercise 1, describe a consistency for each category, regardless of how you view its importance in your own organization. In Step B, you will separate useful consistencies from those that may merely reflect unproductive habits.

EXERCISE 1 WORKSHEET

Identifying Consistencies in People Practices

People Practices	Description of Consistencies
1. Selecting candidates for employment	_____ _____ _____ _____ _____
2. Hiring new employees	_____ _____ _____ _____ _____
3. Indoctrinating new recruits	_____ _____ _____ _____ _____
4. Training employees	_____ _____ _____ _____
5. Evaluating performance of employees	_____ _____ _____ _____
6. Rewarding employees	_____ _____ _____ _____ _____

7. Promoting employees	_____ _____ _____ _____ _____
8. Recognizing outstanding performance	_____ _____ _____ _____
9. Correcting unacceptable performance	_____ _____ _____ _____
10. Terminating employees	_____ _____ _____ _____ _____

IDENTIFYING CONSISTENCIES IN MANAGEMENT PROCESSES

Similar to the preceding one, this exercise turns your attention to your company's management processes. M&M's CEO identified three major consistencies in his company's management processes.

Management Processes	Description of Consistencies
1. Analysis processes	*In the last three years we have become completely consistent in our analysis of potential acquisitions with a step-by-step procedure for determining their soundness. Every acquisition is different, but our analysis process remains the same.*
3. Decision-making processes	*We have been extremely consistent in making decisions about which products we will distribute. Since the nature of the product must match the needs of our customers, we have formulated guidelines that we follow religiously when deciding whether or not to add a new product line.*
7. Management control processes	*We focus heavily and consistently on warehousing and delivery costs and are quite rigid in our cost-control policies.*

Again, as you complete this exercise, don't yet worry about the consequences of a given consistency.

Identifying Consistencies in Management Processes

Management Processes   **Description of Consistencies**

1. Analysis processes

    _____
    _____
    _____
    _____
    _____
    _____
    _____

2. Planning processes

    _____
    _____
    _____
    _____
    _____
    _____

3. Decision-making processes

    _____
    _____
    _____
    _____
    _____
    _____
    _____

4. Organizing processes

    _____
    _____
    _____
    _____
    _____
    _____

5. Implementation processes

    _____
    _____
    _____
    _____
    _____
    _____

6. Communication processes

    _____
    _____
    _____
    _____
    _____

7. Management control processes

    _____
    _____
    _____
    _____
    _____

8. Performance measurement processes

    _____
    _____
    _____
    _____
    _____

9. Reporting processes

    _____
    _____
    _____
    _____
    _____

10. Other processes

    _____
    _____
    _____
    _____
    _____

STEP B

JUDGE THE POSITIVE AND NEGATIVE EFFECTS OF CONSISTENCIES

An organizational consistency can have good or bad consequences. Some consistencies increase productivity by perpetuating commitment and competence within the culture, while others produce harmful effects. In the latter case, the culture may be weak or changing. A company with a consistency that causes negative consequences is like an individual with a habit detrimental to his or her well-being. Just as people find it difficult and even painful to alter bad habits, companies invariably encounter problems when they decide to change a harmful consistency. Cultural adjustments, even for the better, often have a wrenching effect on people. On the other hand, a trend in the marketplace can cause some of an organization's formerly positive consistent practices or processes to become negative. For example, Chase Manhattan Bank has held on to some traditionally positive conservative practices and processes during tremendous changes in its environment and, as a result, has fallen behind its rivals in consumer banking. Now Chase may be tempted to make more culture changes than its people can handle. Since you don't want to replace one bad habit with another, you must proceed with extreme caution as you engage in the next two exercises. Bear in mind that you are still assessing your situation and should not contemplate any adjustments until you get to Chapter 7.

EXERCISE 3
IDENTIFYING THE POSITIVE EFFECTS OF CONSISTENCIES

At this point you will probe the positive effects of each of the consistencies you identified in Exercises 1 and 2, considering each one in turn and looking for positive effects on your company's performance. At M&M Distribution Corporation, the CEO detailed the positive effects for each of the five major consistencies he had identified. Here is a sample of his results:

EXERCISE 3 EXAMPLE

Consistencies	Positive Effects
People Practices	
3. Indoctrinating new recruits: *Indoctrinating new sales people*	*Our sales people are twice as productive as the industry average and new recruits reach peak productivity six months to a year earlier than industry counterparts.*
6. Rewarding employees: *Sales compensation system*	*Our compensation program contributes to the high level of productivity. Furthermore, it motivates sales people to give balanced attention to servicing customers and getting new sales. The balance keeps our customers loyal.*
Management Processes	
1. Analysis processes: *Acquisition analysis*	*Of the 15 acquisitions made over the past three years, only one went sour. Since the other 14 acquisitions fit into our organization, our overall record has been spectacular.*

3. Decision-making processes:
Product selection decisions

Our customers praise our product mix as the best in the industry. This also accounts for their continued loyalty. We have never taken on an unproven product.

7. Management control processes:
Warehouse and delivery cost control

Our warehousing and delivery costs per dollar of sold merchandise are lower than any competitor of similar size. Smaller competitors who achieve lower costs cannot offer our number and mix of products.

Take your time to isolate all the major and minor positive effects of a consistency on your company's performance.

Identifying the Positive Effects of Consistencies

Consistencies   **Positive Effects**

**People
Practices**

1. Selecting
   candidates for
   employment:

   _____

   _____

   _____

2. Hiring new
   employees:

   _____

   _____

3. Indoctrinating
   new recruits:

   _____

   _____

4. Training
   employees:

   _____

   _____

5. Evaluating
   performance of
   employees:

   _____

   _____

   _____

6. Rewarding
   employees:

   _____

   _____

   _____

7. Promoting
   employees:

   _____

   _____

8. Recognizing
   outstanding
   performance:

   _____

   _____

9. Correcting
   unacceptable
   performance:

   _____

   _____

10. Terminating
    employees:

    _____

    _____

Management Processes

1. Analysis processes:

_____

_____

_____

2. Planning processes:

_____

_____

_____

3. Decision-making processes:

_____

_____

_____

4. Organizing processes:

_____

_____

_____

5. Implementation processes:

_____

_____

_____

_____

_____

_____

_____

_____

_____

_____

_____

_____

_____

_____

_____

_____

_____

_____

_____

_____

_____

_____

_____

_____

_____

6. Communication processes:

_____

_____

_____

7. Management control processes:

_____

_____

8. Performance measurement processes:

_____

_____

_____

9. Reporting processes:

_____

_____

10. Other processes:

_____

_____

_____

_____

_____

_____

_____

_____

_____

_____

_____

_____

_____

_____

_____

EXERCISE 4
IDENTIFYING THE NEGATIVE EFFECTS OF CONSISTENCIES

In this exercise you will probe the negative consequences of your consistencies. Remember, if you decide that a given consistency produces negative effects, you will eventually want to make some adjustments in that area, but not until you have considered all the consequences in Chapter 7. In some cases, you may even wish to accept some negative effects if curing them would damage other, more positive, effects. M&M's CEO thought two negative effects might stem from the five major consistencies he had identified. One he was willing to live with, and one he knew would require some change. The two negative effects he found with the help of Exercise 4 follow.

Consistencies	Negative Effects/ Company Position
People Practices	
3. Indoctrinating new recruits: *Indoctrinating new salespeople*	*Many of the existing salespeople within the distribution companies we have acquired refused to conform to our rigid training requirements and, as a consequence, left the company. We have lost some good people but we are not going to modify our training requirements.*
Management Processes	
2. Management control processes: *Warehouse and delivery cost control*	*Our consistent attention to cost control has caused us to be unresponsive to long-range customer needs. Our consistency here has been short range in too many cases.*

As you complete this exercise, include even seemingly small negative effects.

Identifying Negative Effects of Consistencies

Consistencies	Negative Effects/ Company Position

People Practices

1. Selecting candidates for employment:
_____
_____
_____

2. Hiring new employees:
_____
_____
_____

3. Indoctrinating new recruits:
_____
_____

4. Training employees:
_____
_____
_____

5. Evaluating performance of employees:
_____
_____
_____

6. Rewarding employees:
_____
_____
_____

7. Promoting employees:
_____
_____
_____

8. Recognizing outstanding performance:
_____
_____

9. Correcting unacceptable performance:
_____
_____

10. Terminating employees:
_____
_____

135

EXERCISE 4 WORKSHEET (*Cont.*)

Management Processes

1. Analysis processes:

_____
_____
_____

2. Planning processes:

_____
_____
_____

3. Decision-making processes:

_____
_____

4. Organizing processes:

_____
_____

5. Implementation processes:

_____
_____
_____

6. Communication processes:

_____
_____

7. Management control processes:

_____
_____

8. Performance measurement processes:

_____
_____

9. Other processes:

_____
_____

STEP C

DETERMINE WHETHER CONSISTENCIES PERPETUATE COMMITMENT AND COMPETENCE

Now that you have judged both the good and bad consequences of your company's consistencies, you can determine whether your consistencies adequately perpetuate commitment to a common purpose and competence to deliver superior performance. In healthy and productive organizations, commitment, competence, and consistency always stimulate and reinforce one another; consistency functions as a unifying characteristic and helps carry the other two into the future. Positive consistencies are flexible and allow people to adapt quickly and effectively to change, and, like good mission statements, they withstand the test of time. If your consistent people practices and management processes only loosely coincide with your company's commitment and competence, then the strength of your culture will probably deteriorate over the years ahead. A few years ago Safeway lost substantial ground in market leadership and market share when a new CEO failed to consistently perpetuate the company's previously strong commitment to market leadership and a competence for innovative merchandising. Fortunately, the founder's grandson saved the day when he took over the helm and reinstituted the old consistencies. In Exercise 5 you will determine how well consistencies have perpetuated commitment and competence in the past; then in Exercise 6 you will project how well they will do so in the future, as inevitable changes overtake your organization.

EXERCISE 5
ASSESSING THE HISTORICAL VALUE OF CONSISTENCIES

By the time you finish this exercise you will have determined how well your company's consistencies have worked in the past. Each consistency will receive a High, Medium, or Low score, depending on how well it has perpetuated commitment and competence. At M&M Distribution the CEO rated one of his company's consistencies high in terms of building the company's commitment to a common purpose, furthering its dominant competence, and linking commitment and competence together.

EXERCISE 5 EXAMPLE

Consistency: *Indoctrinating New Salespeople*

Rate consistency's value (High, Medium, or Low) in terms of:

a. **Building commitment to the company's common purpose**   *H*
b. **Developing the company's dominant competence**   *H*
c. **Linking commitment and competence together**   *H*

Reasons for ratings: *Our indoctrination program thoroughly stresses the company's basic mission: how we as a company add value to the products we distribute. The indoctrination articulates that purpose and continually builds understanding and commitment. The program also teaches and reinforces basic distribution management skills that deal with warehousing, delivery, distribution information systems, customer service, and cost control. It sets the groundwork for further developing our product distribution expertise and know-how. The program links commitment and competence by constantly communicating that for our company to add value to the products we distribute we must be the most technically expert distributors around. Our people learn from the beginning that commitment and competence go hand in hand.*

Before you assess your own past performance with regard to consistency, review your commitment to a common purpose (Chapter 4) and your dominant competence (Chapter 5). Even if you rated your company's level of commitment or the strength of its dominant competence low, you must still evaluate how it relates to the consistencies you have identified in this chapter, because you will eventually need to know how consistencies perpetuate a weak commitment or a less than superior competence.

Assessing the Historical Value of Consistencies

People Practices

Consistency: _____

_____

Rate consistency's value (High, Medium, or Low) in terms of:

a. Building commitment to your company's common purpose _____

b. Developing your company's dominant competence _____

c. Linking commitment and competence together _____

Reasons for ratings: _____

_____

_____

_____

_____

_____

_____

_____

_____

_____

_____

_____

Consistency: _____

_____

Rate consistency's value (High, Medium, or Low) in terms of:

a. Building commitment to your company's common purpose _____

b. Developing your company's dominant competence _____

c. Linking commitment and competence together _____

Reasons for ratings: _____

_____

_____

_____

_____

_____

_____

_____

_____

Consistency: _____

_____

Rate consistency's value (High, Medium, or Low) in terms of:

a. Building commitment to your company's common purpose _____

b. Developing your company's dominant competence _____

c. Linking commitment and competence together _____

Reasons for ratings: _____

_____

_____

_____

_____

_____

_____

_____

_____

_____

EXERCISE 5 WORKSHEET (*Cont.*)

Consistency: _____
_____

Rate consistency's value (High, Medium, or Low) in terms of:

   a. **Building commitment to your company's common purpose** _____
   b. **Developing your company's dominant competence** _____
   c. **Linking commitment and competence together** _____

Reasons for ratings: _____
_____
_____
_____
_____
_____
_____
_____
_____
_____
_____
_____

Consistency: _____
_____

Rate consistency's value (High, Medium, or Low) in terms of:

   a. **Building commitment to your company's common purpose** _____
   b. **Developing your company's dominant competence** _____
   c. **Linking commitment and competence together** _____

Reasons for ratings: _____
_____
_____
_____
_____
_____
_____
_____
_____
_____
_____
_____

Consistency: _____
_____

Rate consistency's value (High, Medium, or Low) in terms of:

   a. **Building commitment to your company's common purpose** _____
   b. **Developing your company's dominant competence** _____
   c. **Linking commitment and competence together** _____

Reasons for ratings: _____
_____
_____
_____
_____
_____
_____
_____
_____

Consistency: _____
_____

Rate consistency's value (High, Medium, or Low) in terms of:

   a. **Building commitment to your company's common purpose** _____
   b. **Developing your company's dominant competence** _____
   c. **Linking commitment and competence together** _____

Reasons for ratings: _____
_____
_____
_____
_____
_____
_____
_____
_____

Consistency: _____

_____

Rate consistency's value (High, Medium, or Low) in terms of:

  a. **Building commitment to your company's common purpose** _____

  b. **Developing your company's dominant competence** _____

  c. **Linking commitment and competence together** _____

Reasons for ratings: _____

_____

_____

_____

_____

_____

_____

_____

_____

_____

_____

_____

_____

Consistency: _____

_____

Rate consistency's value (High, Medium, or Low) in terms of:

  a. **Building commitment to your company's common purpose** _____

  b. **Developing your company's dominant competence** _____

  c. **Linking commitment and competence together** _____

Reasons for ratings: _____

_____

_____

_____

_____

_____

_____

_____

_____

_____

_____

_____

_____

Consistency: _____

_____

Rate consistency's value (High, Medium, or Low) in terms of:

  a. **Building commitment to your company's common purpose** _____

  b. **Developing your company's dominant competence** _____

  c. **Linking commitment and competence together** _____

Reasons for ratings: _____

_____

_____

_____

_____

_____

_____

_____

_____

_____

_____

_____

PROJECTING THE FUTURE VALUE OF CONSISTENCIES

Finally you can turn your analysis of consistencies toward the future, describing how continued consistencies will affect and be affected by new directions or trends both inside and outside your organization. M&M's CEO identified one consistency he felt should not continue:

EXERCISE 6 EXAMPLE

Consistencies	**What Will Happen in the Future if This Consistency Continues?**
Warehouse and delivery cost control	*Our consistent short-range cost-controlling view may need to be supplemented with greater responsiveness to our customers' long-range needs. If we fail to respond to longer-range needs with early planning, we may lose our hard-won customer loyalty to more forward-looking competitors. We may need to add another consistency.*

Just as the M&M CEO did, you should build detailed scenarios that project the future consequences of each consistency.

EXERCISE 6 WORKSHEET
Projecting the Future Value of Consistencies

What Will Happen in the Future if This Consistency Continues?

Consistency:

_____

_____

Consistency:

_____

_____

Consistency:

_____

_____

Consistency:

_____

_____

Consistency:

_____

_____

EXERCISE 6 WORKSHEET (*Cont.*)

Consistency:

_____

_____

Consistency:

_____

_____

Consistency:

_____

_____

Consistency:

_____

_____

Consistency:

_____

_____

SUMMARY

You can now record your conclusions from this chapter. Before you start, consider some of the conclusions the M&M CEO drew as he summarized his responses to all six exercises (see next column).

SUMMARY EXAMPLE

Part A

Conclusions from Step A, Exercises 1 and 2

Our consistency in people practices only focuses on salespeople, and although they make up two-thirds of our work force, we need to refine our practices with our other people.

Part B

Conclusions from Step B, Exercises 3 and 4

While we identified only one negative effect, it is a major one because it deals with customer responsiveness.

Part C

Conclusions from Step C, Exercises 5 and 6

Our indoctrination practices for new salespeople, effectively perpetuate our company's commitment and competence.

Part D

Overall Summary of Conclusions

The consistencies which our company exhibits are strong, but we need to orient them more toward the long-term needs of our customers.

Part E

Future Directions

Perhaps we can conduct a focus-group retreat with our major buyers, asking them to project their own missions five, ten, or fifteen years into the future. Their long-range missions will influence our own long-range mission.

Spend some extra time brainstorming ideas for the future directions.

SUMMARY WORKSHEET

Part A

Conclusions from Step A, Exercises 1 and 2, pages 127–129

1. _____

_____

_____

_____

2. _____

_____

_____

_____

3. _____

_____

_____

Part B

Conclusions from Step B, Exercises 3 and 4, pages 132–136

1. _____

_____

_____

2. _____

_____

_____

3. _____

_____

_____

Part C

Conclusions from Step C, Exercises 5 and 6, pages 139–144

1. _____

_____

_____

_____

2. _____

_____

_____

3. _____

_____

_____

Part D

Overall Summary of Conclusions

1. _____

_____

_____

2. _____

_____

3. _____

_____

4. _____

_____

_____

5. _____
_____
_____
_____
_____
_____

6. _____
_____
_____
_____
_____
_____

Part E
Future Directions

_____
_____
_____
_____
_____
_____
_____
_____
_____
_____
_____
_____
_____
_____
_____
_____
_____

At last you have finished the arduous assessment of your strategy-culture alloy and can finally pull together all you have learned. In the next chapter and then in Part II of the workbook you will begin to transform your insights into action.

CHAPTER 7

PUTTING IT ALL TOGETHER

The best executives may act decisively, but they always "think before they leap." For two decades Citicorp's visionary leader, Walter Wriston, thought deeply about the future of banking and then revolutionized a whole industry as he pushed banks into a host of new businesses. The power of Wriston's intellectual leadership has prompted many banking executives to "leap" after him and strive to follow his lead in innovatively offering a full range of financial services.

But one maverick thinker has a mind of his own. Charles S. Sanford, Jr., president of Bankers Trust, chose to rethink his company's competitive position rather than blindly imitate Citicorp. Sanford concluded that only a few of the largest competitors, such as Citicorp or Bank of America, could create lasting excellence by adopting Wriston's ideas. Sanford decided to carve a narrower niche for Bankers Trust, creating a hybrid institution that united commercial and investment banking but completely abandoned consumer services. This radical new direction brought impressive results in 1984 as Bankers Trust earned $16.20 for every $100 of equity, outdistancing the fourteen largest holding companies in the industry.

Like other execupreneurs, Sanford not only rethought his company's strategy, he rethought its culture, further implementing the changes begun by his predecessor, Alfred Brittain III. Brittain shocked the financial community by forcing out veteran employees who were unable to adjust to his demands for creativity and productivity and rewarding his people not on the traditional basis of seniority but solely on the basis of merit. Under Brittain, senior management was expected to behave like partners rather than like the stewards of their own special fiefdoms. This cultural shift, combined with Sanford's new strategic direction, has propelled Bankers Trust to the ranks of the most profitable and admired organizations in its field.

So far you have been doing a lot of thinking about your own strategy and culture, and if you have carefully completed all the exercises in the preceding chapters, you have created a detailed audit of the current components of your strategy-culture alloy, an assessment that should provide one integrated picture on which you can base decisions to bolster your strategy, your culture, or both. Although Part II of this workbook focuses on taking action, the effectiveness of your eventual action will depend both on the thoroughness of your analysis in Part I and on your ability to think through the consequences of changes you might make in any of the six strategy-culture components.

To accurately predict the outcome of any change and its impact on all the other strategy-culture factors, you will again take three crucial steps:

Step A: **Measure the benefits of new strategic directions**

Step B: **Evaluate the benefits of new cultural traits**

Step C: **Determine the match between new strategic and cultural elements**

The first two steps involve the overall conclusions and future directions you recorded at the ends of Chapters 1–3 (strategy) and Chapters 4–6 (culture), while the third involves learning how to use a simple but powerful new tool, the Strategy-Culture Matching Grid.

STEP A

MEASURE THE BENEFITS OF NEW STRATEGIC DIRECTIONS

Before you can judge the consequences of an adjustment to one of the three strategy factors (satisfying customer needs, sustaining a competitive advantage, and capitalizing on company strengths), you must articulate your company's current strategy and predict where it will most likely take you in the future. Then you can review your responses to the exercises in the strategy chapters, paying particular attention to the sections on overall conclusions and future directions. If your brainstorming at the end of each chapter gave you some insights into possible adjustments, you will want to think through their consequences before you actually take any action. You should consider each strategy factor in turn.

EXERCISE 1
DESCRIBING THE CONSEQUENCES OF YOUR CURRENT STRATEGY

In this exercise you want to write a clear sentence or paragraph articulating your current efforts with respect to customers, competitors, and company strengths. With such descriptions in mind, you can construct scenarios forecasting where adherence to your current efforts will take you in the future. Look back at the example companies we discussed in Chapters 1–3. In the case of Landon Corporation, the sign-making firm in Chapter 1, Phil Landon wrote the following description of his current strategy with respect to satisfying customer needs.

EXERCISE 1 EXAMPLE

1. **How does your company satisfy customer needs?**
   A. **Current effort:** *We aggressively market our ability to produce high-quality, dependable signs on a strict timetable.*
   B. **Probable consequences:** *Unless we do a better job of determining needs according to the purpose of our customers' signs, we will lose customers. No matter how high the quality of a sign is, if it doesn't get the job done, it fails to satisfy a need.*

As you complete this exercise, keep in mind that you are still dealing with current, not future, strategy. In the first three chapters you may have drawn conclusions that led you to develop ideas about future directions, but delay your consideration of those changes until Exercise 3.

Describing the Consequences of Your Current Strategy

1. How does your company satisfy customer needs?

   A. Current effort: _____
   _____
   _____
   _____

   B. Probable consequences: _____
   _____
   _____
   _____
   _____
   _____

2. How does your company sustain competitive advantage?

   A. Current effort: _____
   _____
   _____
   _____

   B. Probable consequences: _____
   _____
   _____
   _____
   _____
   _____

3. How does your company capitalize on its strengths?

   A. Current effort: _____
   _____
   _____
   _____

   B. Probable consequences: _____
   _____
   _____
   _____
   _____
   _____

EXERCISE 2
RATING YOUR CURRENT STRATEGY

With an understanding of the consequences in mind, you can calculate a rating for your company's overall strategy by combining ratings for each strategy component. We have designed a rating system that will enable you to place your strategy somewhere on a continuum between excellent and unacceptable. Points are awarded according to something like an academic grading system, with A representing excellent, B representing good, C representing satisfactory, D representing poor, and F representing unacceptable.

A+	=	12 points
A	=	11 points
A−	=	10 points
B+	=	9 points
B	=	8 points
B−	=	7 points
C+	=	6 points
C	=	5 points
C−	=	4 points
D+	=	3 points
D	=	2 points
D−	=	1 point
F	=	0 points

Looking back at the newspaper example in Chapter 3, you will recall that the company's management concluded that it had done a good job of capitalizing on its design strength. Therefore, management's response to item 3 of the exercise looked like the example in the next column.

EXERCISE 2 EXAMPLE

3. **Grade the success of your company's strategy in terms of capitalizing on company strengths:**

   Grade __*A*__   Points __11__

   Rationale for grade: *The strategy draws upon strong internal capabilities that brought about such strengths as "newspaper design and concept innovations," as well as others.*

Combining this score with scores for satisfying customers (Grade B, 8 points) and sustaining a competitive advantage (Grade A−, 10 points), management arrived at a total score of 29. Its strategy bordered on excellence:

4. **Total score:** __29__

Although your own rating will reflect a qualitative judgment based upon what you know and how you feel about your company's strategy, you can make it more objective by considering how your *customers* would rate your company's success in meeting their needs, how your *competitors* would rate your ability to sustain competitive advantage, and how your *employees* would rate how well you capitalize on company strengths.

Rating Your Current Strategy

1. **Grade the success of your company's strategy in terms of satisfying customer needs:**

   Grade _____   Points _____

   Rationale for grade:

2. **Grade the success of your company's strategy in terms of sustaining competitive advantage:**

   Grade _____   Points _____

   Rationale for grade:

3. **Grade the success of your company's strategy in terms of capitalizing on company strengths:**

   Grade _____   Points _____

   Rationale for grade:

4. **Total score:** _____

   Mark your point score on the continuum:

```
36  33  30  27  24  21  18  15  12   9   6   3   0
|                   |           |           |
Excellent         Good      Satisfactory   Poor  Unacceptable
```

EXERCISE 3

PROJECTING THE RESULTS OF CHANGES BASED ON YOUR OVERALL CONCLUSIONS AND FUTURE DIRECTIONS FROM CHAPTERS 1–3

In this exercise you will review your overall conclusions and ideas about future directions from each strategy chapter before forecasting the consequences of any possible change in a strategy factor. To make such projections, you need to construct fairly detailed scenarios describing the likely impact a given change will have on either satisfying customers, sustaining competitive advantage, or capitalizing on company strengths.

A good scenario should take into account immediate implications as well as those one, five, or even ten years in the future. Though a change in one factor affects all other strategy and culture factors, at this stage you should restrict your thinking to a thorough scenario for each factor in turn. Later you will learn how to anticipate the complex relationships among the factors in a dynamic organization.

The national discount-store chain from Chapter 2 built its scenario for a change in competitive advantage as per the example in the next column.

---

2. **The results of a change in the way you sustain competitive advantage:**
   A. **Possible change:**   *Sustain competitive advantage by enhancing our credit card program to include a wide variety of financial services, including automated tellers, discount incentives for card charges, and access to a local bank's full services.*
   B. **Immediate impact:**   *We would incur substantial first-year start-up costs, but much less than a competitor starting from scratch. However, we could offer some enhancements, such as special discount sales for current cardholders only and perhaps increase their number 5–10% by the end of the year.*
   C. **1-to-10-year scenario:**   *We must study all enhancements to decide which we should implement immediately and which we should phase into the program over a 5-year period. New enhancements should respond to competitor's efforts to catch up, thus keeping us always 1–5 years ahead of them. This way, we can sustain this advantage for at least 10 years.*

When you construct your own projections, try to quantify results as much as possible, estimating percentage increases and specific time frames.

Projecting the Results of Changes Based on Your Overall Conclusions and Future Directions from Chapters 1–3

1. **The results of a change in the way you satisfy customers:**

   A. Possible change: _____
   _____
   _____
   _____
   _____

   B. Immediate impact: _____
   _____
   _____
   _____
   _____

   C. 1-to-10-year scenario: _____
   _____
   _____
   _____
   _____

2. **The results of a change in the way you sustain competitive advantage:**

   A. Possible change: _____
   _____
   _____
   _____

   B. Immediate impact: _____
   _____
   _____
   _____

   C. 1-to-10-year scenario: _____
   _____
   _____
   _____

3. **The results of a change in the way you capitalize on strengths:**

   A. Possible change: _____
   _____
   _____
   _____

   B. Immediate impact: _____
   _____
   _____
   _____

   C. 1-to-10-year scenario: _____
   _____
   _____
   _____

STEP B

EVALUATE THE BENEFITS OF NEW CULTURAL TRAITS

Now you can examine the future of your company's culture, first rating its current overall performance and then projecting the results of altering any aspect of it. First you will project the probable consequences of maintaining the status quo, then you will grade the status quo and estimate the implications of acting on the conclusions and future directions from Chapters 4, 5, and 6.

EXERCISE 4
DESCRIBING THE CONSEQUENCES OF YOUR CURRENT CULTURE

As in Exercise 1, you need to write a clear sentence or paragraph characterizing your current efforts with respect to commitment to a common purpose, competence to deliver superior performance, and consistency in perpetuating commitment and competence. And, as you did before, you will build scenarios that project the probable consequences of sticking with current cultural traits.

In Chapter 4 we watched a computer company, JCN, wrestle with its mission statement and commitment. Observe how JCN's management filled out a portion of this present exercise:

EXERCISE 4 EXAMPLE

1. **What common purpose drives your company's commitment?**
   A. **Your commitment to a common purpose:** *We will knowledgeably deliver the most innovative and advanced computer technology to technically sophisticated customers, thereby supporting our customers' innovations and providingour people with the satisfaction and financial rewards of enhancing our customers' accomplishments.*
   B. **Notable exceptions (from Chapter 4, Exercise 3):** *Our research scientists lack customer and profitability awareness.*
   C. **Probable consequences:** *If our scientists' lack of customer and profitability awareness persists, we will see our research budgets continue to increase, even in areas with no tangible customer benefits, and we could suffer an unacceptable erosion of earnings and the loss of customers to competitors who*

tailor their products more closely to customer needs.

As you complete this exercise for your own corporate culture, bear in mind that you are still dealing with current, not future, cultural traits. In Exercise 6 you will be able to forecast the likely results of any changes you might make based on your overall conclusions and future directions at the ends of Chapters 4–6.

Describing the Consequences of Your Current Culture

1. **What common purpose drives your company's commitment?**

   A. **Your commitment to a common purpose:** _____
      _____
      _____
      _____
      _____
      _____

   B. **Notable exceptions (from Chapter 4, Exercise 3):** _____
      _____
      _____
      _____
      _____
      _____

   C. **Probable consequences:** _____
      _____
      _____
      _____
      _____
      _____

2. **What dominant competence has your company developed?**

   A. **Summary of dominant competence:** _____
      _____
      _____
      _____
      _____

   B. **Probable consequences:** _____
      _____
      _____
      _____
      _____
      _____

3. **How consistently do you perpetuate commitment and competence?**

   A. **Summary of consistencies:** _____
      _____
      _____
      _____
      _____
      _____

   B. **Probable consequences:** _____
      _____
      _____
      _____
      _____
      _____

RATING YOUR CURRENT CULTURE

Using the same sort of grading system you employed in Exercise 2, you can now rate each of your current culture's traits, combining the ratings for each into an overall score that will allow you to place your culture on a continuum somewhere between strong and weak. Again:

A+	=	12 points
A	=	11 points
A−	=	10 points
B+	=	9 points
B	=	8 points
B−	=	7 points
C+	=	6 points
C	=	5 points
C−	=	4 points
D+	=	3 points
D	=	2 points
D−	=	1 point
F	=	0 points

On question 2, MWP, the Midwestern utility company from Chapter 5, rated its culture in the following way.

2. How do you rate the strength of your company's competence to deliver superior performance?

Grade ___ *B−* ___   Points ___ *7* ___

Rationale for grade: *Although we have become quite skilled at handling our relationships with regulatory agencies and resolving crises, our defensive posture has exacerbated an adversarial relationship with our customers.*

MWP's management rated commitment to a common purpose somewhat higher (Grade B+, 9 points) but consistency much lower (Grade C, 5 points) because it felt its people received "mixed signals" from managers who tended to pay lip service to customer orientation but reward defensive tactics:

4. Total score: ___ *21* ___

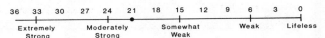

36	33	30	27	24	21	18	15	12	9	6	3	0

Extremely Strong   Moderately Strong   Somewhat Weak   Weak   Lifeless

To make your own judgments as objective as possible, ask the following questions: How would your company's *employees* rate their commitment to a common purpose? How would outside *observers, customers,* and *competitors* rate your dominant competence? How would your company's *management team* rate your consistency in perpetuating commitment and competence?

EXERCISE 5 WORKSHEET

Rating Your Current Culture

1. **How do you rate the strength of your company's commitment to a common purpose?**

   Grade _____   **Points** _____

   Rationale for grade: _____

   _____

   _____

   _____

2. **How do you rate the strength of your company's competence to deliver superior performance?**

   Grade _____   **Points** _____

   Rationale for grade: _____

   _____

   _____

   _____

3. **How do you rate your company's consistency in perpetuating commitment and competence?**

   Grade _____   **Points** _____

   Rationale for grade: _____

   _____

   _____

   _____

4. **Total score:** _____

   Mark your point score on the continuum:

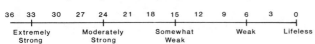

| 36 | 33 | 30 | 27 | 24 | 21 | 18 | 15 | 12 | 9 | 6 | 3 | 0 |

Extremely Strong   Moderately Strong   Somewhat Weak   Weak   Lifeless

EXERCISE 6

PROJECTING THE RESULTS OF CHANGES BASED ON YOUR OVERALL CONCLUSIONS AND FUTURE DIRECTIONS FROM CHAPTERS 4–6

Similar to Exercise 4, this exercise asks you to review your overall conclusions from each culture chapter and then build scenarios that will test the results of any possible change you might make with respect to the three cultural traits: commitment, competence, and consistency.

M&M Distribution from Chapter 6 forecast the results from a potential change in its consistency (see the example in the next column).

EXERCISE 6 EXAMPLE

3. **The results of a change in the way you consistently perpetuate commitment and competence:**
   A. **Possible change:** *Inaugurate a planning process that stresses more attention to our customers' long-range needs while still enforcing our strict warehousing and delivery cost-control policies.*
   B. **Immediate impact:** *Our customers would appreciate our new attention to their own strategies for growth and would reward our attention with even greater loyalty.*
   C. **1-to-10-year scenario:** *We would be caught with fewer shortages of products, the demand for which springs from a trend or fashion change, and we would even be able to help our customers take better advantage of such changes. This consistency would have a lasting, ongoing benefit for our customers and ourselves.*

Your own scenarios should track the results of changes one to ten years into the future.

Projecting the Results of Changes Based on Your Overall Conclusions and Future Directions from Chapters 4–6

1. The results of changes in your commitment to a common purpose:

   A. Possible change: _____
   _____
   _____
   _____
   _____

   B. Immediate impact: _____
   _____
   _____
   _____
   _____

   C. 1-to-10-year scenario: _____
   _____
   _____
   _____
   _____

2. The results of a change in your overriding competence:

   A. Possible change: _____
   _____
   _____
   _____
   _____

   B. Immediate impact: _____
   _____
   _____
   _____
   _____

   C. 1-to-10-year scenario: _____
   _____
   _____
   _____
   _____

3. The results of a change in the way you consistently perpetuate commitment and competence:

   A. Possible change: _____
   _____
   _____
   _____
   _____

   B. Immediate impact: _____
   _____
   _____
   _____
   _____

   C. 1-to-10-year scenario: _____
   _____
   _____
   _____
   _____

STEP C

DETERMINE THE MATCH BETWEEN NEW STRATEGIC AND CULTURAL ELEMENTS

Once you have rated your company's current strategy and culture and projected the likely results of a change in any one of their six components, you must determine how a given change might relate to and affect all the others. The excellent organization always integrates its strategy with its culture, making sure they support each other. Since a change in one area can have tremendous impact on another area, even a slight mismatch can throw off the entire balance.

When we set about the arduous task of forging an ideal alloy from a brilliant strategy and a strong culture, we began by carefully analyzing the six factors that contribute to excellence. The three strategic factors aim at getting and keeping customers, while the three culture factors aim at attracting, developing, motivating, and unifying employees. When a strategy to get and keep customers requires employees to act and think in unaccustomed ways, employees may respond poorly or even feel resentful. On the other hand, no matter how effectively a culture may motivate and develop employees, if customers do not perceive better products and services as a result, the culture will be wasted. The intertwined relationship between customers and employees requires watchful management because, like pieces of a complicated jigsaw puzzle, each component of an internally consistent strategy must fit snugly with each trait of a robust and productive culture.

Given what can be a complex and even intimidating range of relationships among the six strategy-culture factors, we have devised the following Strategy-Culture Matching Grid to help you simplify the problem.

CULTURE

STRATEGY	Cultivating Commitment to a Common Purpose	Developing Competence to Deliver Superior Performance	Perpetuating Commitment and Competence Through Consistency
Satisfying Customer Needs	*Match?*	*Match?*	*Match?*
Sustaining Competitive Advantage	*Match?*	*Match?*	*Match?*
Capitalizing on Company Strengths	*Match?*	*Match?*	*Match?*

This chart makes clear the nine different combinations among the factors that you should consider when you wish to understand the effects a given change in either strategy or culture will have on your organization. Strong matches among all nine combinations indicate an excellent strategy-culture alloy. You can use this powerful tool four ways:

1. By placing your current set of strategy-culture factors in the grid, you'll gain a broad perspective on your current situation and the existing match between strategy and culture.
2. Whenever you contemplate a change in one of the six factors, you can test the impact of that change throughout your organization.
3. You can thoroughly evaluate a major overhaul of strategy or culture or both.
4. You can regularly use it to "take the temperature" of your company's strategy-culture alloy, even if your company enjoys excellence at the moment.

Exercise 7 will help add a great deal of detail to the consequences you described in Exercises 1 and 4; Exercise 8 will prepare you for taking action by helping you test the effects of any possible changes you are considering. Long-range results with long-range scenarios were projected in Exercises 3 and 6; in Exercise 7 you will be fleshing out these results in considerable detail. By the end of the exercise you will have fully graded your organization's strategy and culture. You graded your company's current strategy in Exercise 2 and your current culture in Exercise 5; in Exercise 7 you will grade the current *match* between strategy and culture.

Finally, Exercise 8 provides a transition to Part II, where you will begin to take corrective action aimed at improving your strategy, culture, and strategy-culture alloy. As you determine the matches or mismatches that might occur if you make a certain change, you will be able to preview the likely outcomes of that action. In Part II, you will not only explore such outcomes more deeply, you will observe how actual companies have improved their own alloys and learn from their experiences.

EXERCISE 7
USING THE STRATEGY-CULTURE MATCHING GRID

First you'll apply the Strategy-Culture Matching Grid to your company's current strategy and culture. Before you begin, observe how the electric utility from Chapter 5 did it. Midwest Power had written the following descriptions of its current strategy and culture in Exercises 1 and 4:

Strategy

Satisfying customer needs: *We meet customers' needs by providing reliable electrical service and helping them control energy costs with new service and product alternatives.*

Sustaining competitive advantage: *We maintain an advantage over competitors by assuming an energy leadership position in the midst of technical and regulatory change, initiating products and services that are better than competitors'.*

Capitalizing on company strengths: *We enjoy a rich base of technical, energy-related resources and abilities we can exploit to create new and better services and products for customers.*

Culture

Commitment to a common purpose: *The company's current mission is survival in a changing industry and world.*

Competence to deliver superior performance: *The company's dominant competence is the effective management of all public, political, legislative, and regulatory relationships to successfully defend its position.*

Consistency in perpetuating commitment and competence: *The company consistently recognizes and rewards the crisis resolution behavior that perpetuates the commitment to survival and the*

competence at defending the company's position.

A year earlier, MWP had embarked on a new strategy. Faced with increasingly hostile customers, growing competition from alternative energy sources, such as passive solar power, and a relaxed regulatory environment demanding innovation rather than defensive legal and political maneuvering, the company had decided to recapture its former leadership position by investing heavily in new products and services. Unfortunately, since the culture still maintained its old defensive traits, MWP found many mismatches when it used the matching grid and the scoring system from Exercises 2 and 5.

CULTURE

STRATEGY	Commitment to Survival	Competence in Managing External Relationships to Defend Company	Consistent Recognition and Reward of Crisis Resolution Behavior
Meet Customer Needs Through Reliable Service and New Product Service Alternatives	Grade: __B__ __8__ Points	Grade: __C−__ __4__ Points	Grade: __C__ __5__ Points
Assume Leadership Position by Developing Better Services and Products	Grade: __B−__ __7__ Points	Grade: __D__ __2__ Points	Grade: __D+__ __3__ Points
Exploit Technical Strengths to Offer New Services and Products and Enter New Businesses	Grade: __C__ __5__ Points	Grade: __D__ __2__ Points	Grade: __D+__ __3__ Points

Total Score ___39___   Overall Grade ___C−___   *(39 ÷ 9 = 4.3)*

Since MWP's management decided that the new strategy was essential to the long-term well-being of the utility, it concluded that the mismatches arose from the fact that its strong defensive culture was weak with respect to the company's new direction. (MWP had graded its strategy an "A," its culture a "B−," and the match a "C−.") Therefore, management classified the organization as having a sound strategy but lacking the sort of culture needed to implement the strategy. Any organization with a strong, albeit mismatched, culture like MWP's should embark with extreme caution on any new strategy requiring a major change in the culture. In MWP's case the strong defensive culture had helped the company survive past threats, but it was preventing management from making important changes that could guarantee success in the future. As indicated in Exercise 5, MWP rated its commitment much higher than the other two components of culture. Therefore MWP's best matches between strategy and culture appeared between commitment and each of the three strategy factors. The culture did feel committed to survival, a condition that would certainly help implement a new strategy. However, a new dominant competence and a new set of consistencies will be required before MWP can achieve excellence.

Now you can apply the Strategy-Culture Matching Grid to your own current situation. After grading all nine matches, record your total score, then divide by nine to arrive at your overall grade.

Using the Strategy-Culture Matching Grid

CULTURE

STRATEGY	Cultivating Commitment to a Common Purpose	Developing Competence to Deliver Superior Performance	Perpetuating Commitment and Competence through Consistency
Satisfying Customer Needs _____ _____ _____ _____ _____	Grade: _____ _____ Points	Grade: _____ _____ Points	Grade: _____ _____ Points
Sustaining Competitive Advantage _____ _____ _____ _____	Grade: _____ _____ Points	Grade: _____ _____ Points	Grade: _____ _____ Points
Capitalizing on Company Strengths _____ _____ _____ _____ _____	Grade: _____ _____ Points	Grade: _____ _____ Points	Grade: _____ _____ Points

Total Score _____   Overall Grade _____

EXERCISE 8
PREPARING FOR ACTION

Once you have tested your current situation with the matching grid, you can begin to preview the results of future changes. Remember that the grid is a tool. Play with it, run your wildest ideas through it, and get so familiar with it that it becomes a mental habit. As you experiment, test one change at a time; otherwise, this simple tool can quickly grow cumbersome.

MWP's management experimented with the following ideas, as recorded in Exercises 3 and 6:

Strategy

1. Customers: *Maintain our current strategy.*

2. Competitors: *Maintain our current strategy.*

3. Company strengths: *Maintain our current strategy.*

Culture

1. Commitment: *Implement company-wide indoctrination/educational program designed to augment the company's commitment to survival to include a commitment to remaining the market leader by serving customers better and not treating them like enemies.*

2. Competence: *Institute customer-service training programs and stress innovation of alternatives.*

3. Consistency: *Recognize and reward people on the basis of positive customer relations and innovation of alternatives.*

CULTURE

STRATEGY	Commitment to Market Leadership	Competence in Customer Service and Innovation	Consistent Recognition and Rewards for Customer Service and Innovation
Satisfying Customer Needs	Grade: _B+_ _9_ Points	Grade: _B−_ _7_ Points	Grade: _A_ _11_ Points
Sustaining Competitive Advantage	Grade: _B−_ _7_ Points	Grade: _B_ _8_ Points	Grade: _A_ _11_ Points
Capitalizing on Company Strengths	Grade: _A−_ _10_ Points	Grade: _B+_ _9_ Points	Grade: _A_ _11_ Points

Total Score _83_   Overall Grade _B+_

As MWP's management ran the three changes, one by one, through the grid, the executives soon saw that each change would improve the matches between strategy and culture factors. Although the preceding grid shows the results of all three changes, the company actually performed the experiment three separate times, evaluating each change individually.

Notice that the grade improved, but not to an overall A. As management previewed the import of each change, it realized that the reeducation and retraining would take considerable time because people would find it difficult to substitute a new set of strong traits for the old set. Only after rewards had reinforced the new traits would people begin to fully "buy in" to the new program. Likewise, the effects of the changes would first affect capitalizing on company strengths, then satisfying customer needs, and, finally, sustaining competitive advantage.

Be freewheeling, creative, and execupreneurial at this point. Since you're not yet acting on any potential changes, you can learn the most from a brainstorming approach. We have designed the following Strategy-Culture Matching Grid so you can photocopy it for use by all the people you want to get involved in this exercise.

EXERCISE 8 WORKSHEET

Preparing for Action

STRATEGY	CULTURE		
	Cultivating Commitment to a Common Purpose	Developing Competence to Deliver Superior Performance	Perpetuating Commitment and Competence through Consistency
Satisfying Customer Needs			
Sustaining Competitive Advantage			
Capitalizing on Company Strengths			

PART II

INTRODUCTION

Once you have mastered the use of the matching grid you can launch into an action program. Each of the following chapters will deal with one of four classic organizational types: Type A companies, with excellent strategies and strong cultures; Type B companies, with strong cultures but weak strategies; Type C companies, with strong strategies but weak cultures; and Type D companies, with weak strategies and weak cultures. Although the A, B, C, D classifications, like the rating system introduced in Chapter 7, help you get a firmer grasp on your situation, they are, by their very nature, somewhat arbitrary. In the real world the attributes of an organization defy such easy compartmentalization. Therefore, as you proceed with the following chapters you will see a rich range of examples in each category and you will learn how to adjust your actions to suit a variety of situations. Since you may someday move to another company, and since any company you work for will certainly evolve over the years, you can profit from studying all four chapters. However, you will probably want to zero in on the type that most closely parallels your own current situation.

Before you begin, you should use your strategy and culture ratings from Chapter 7 (Exercises 2 and 5) to classify your own organization as one of the classic types. Note that your classification depends on the individual grades you gave your company's strategy and culture, not the overall grade you gave the match between strategy and culture. You will want to take into account what you learned from your initial use of the Strategy-Culture Matching Grid because you are striving not just for a brilliant strategy and a strong culture but a healthy match between the two. As we saw earlier with the utility company example, MWP, its strategy and culture grades were both higher than its matching grade. In the next few pages you will use your own strategy and culture grades to classify your organization; then you will have the opportunity in the following chapters to use the Strategy-Culture Matching Grid once again to help you make the kind of match between strategy and culture that creates excellence. Remember, congruence, not just strategic and cultural strength, leads to excellence.

Although you should already have a pretty good idea about the category that best describes your present situation, you will want to position yourself more precisely. Every company is unique and no situation is ever black or white. The Organizational Classification Chart will help you determine the relative shades of gray that apply to your organization.

To get a feel for using this chart to rate your own situation, consider how the example companies from Chapters 1–6 used it. In Chapter 7 they awarded themselves the following ratings:

- Landon Corporation, the signage company, (Chapter 1) rated its strategy 15, its culture 27.
- The National Discount Chain (Chapter 2) rated its strategy 21, its culture 15.
- The Newspaper (Chapter 3) rated its strategy 33, its culture 30.
- JCN, the computer company (Chapter 4), rated its strategy 33, its culture 21.
- The Midwestern utility, MWP (Chapter 5), rated its strategy 34, its culture 21.
- M&M Distribution (Chapter 6) rated its strategy 8, its culture 30.

Then each firm plotted its relative position on the following Organizational Classification Chart.

ORGANIZATIONAL CLASSIFICATION CHART

STRATEGY   CULTURE

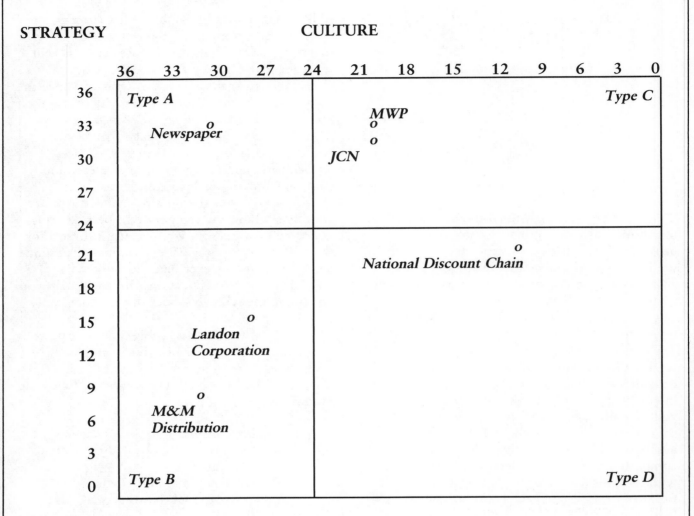

Clearly, each of these companies faces its own unique set of problems. As we will see in the following chapters, a Type A company, such as the newspaper, may try to refine both its strategy and culture, but it will undoubtedly pay more attention to maintaining its alloy than tinkering with it. Since organizations always find it harder to improve culture than strategy, the Type C's (JCN and MWP) face a more difficult task than the Type B's (Landon and M&M). And the discount chain, as a Type D, obviously faces the most difficult challenge.

Using your strategy and culture ratings from Chapter 7 (Exercises 2 and 5), plot your own organization on the chart.

ORGANIZATIONAL CLASSIFICATION CHART

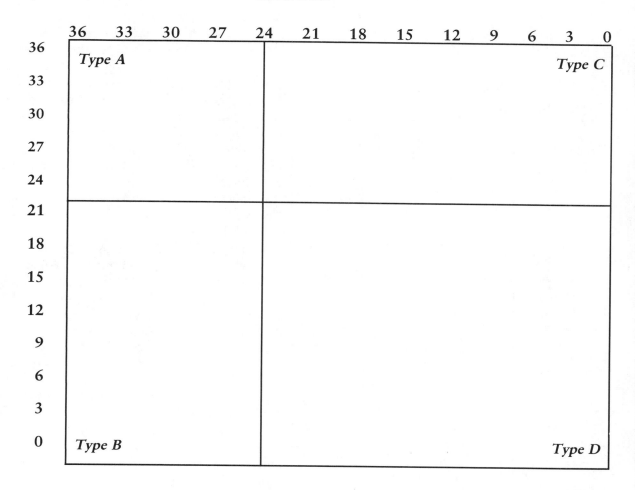

As you proceed with the following chapters, you will want to keep your final assessments from Chapter 7 firmly in mind. Each examination of an organization type will begin with some general background, including examples of well-known companies that we believe now fall, or once fell, into the category. With these historical examples as a backdrop, we will then discuss some specific ways you can successfully manage such a situation.

Each chapter's Action Plans section provides three exercises designed to help you plan the step-by-step measures you can take to improve or maintain your position. The results you predicted for changes in strategy (Chapter 7, Exercise 3) and culture (Chapter 7, Exercise 6), and the insights you gained from working with the Strategy-Culture Matching Grid (Chapter 7, Exercises 7 and 8), should form the general basis for your Action Plans. For each organizational type you will design a preliminary plan, test it with the Strategy-Culture Matching Grid, and then finalize the changes that will help you create a more prosperous future for your company.

Whether you study all of the following chapters or just focus on the one that most closely parallels your own situation, you will want to put your best thinking into the effort. By its very nature, this workbook has compartmentalized the components of excellence and has followed a fairly rigid step-by-step approach; but companies are complicated, fluid, dynamic organisms and their successful management requires the brain power and creativity of what we call the execupreneur.

8

TYPE D ORGANIZATIONS

Type D organizations suffer from such weak cultures and bad strategies that they often seek protection under Chapter 11 bankruptcy laws; their financial statements always display marginal profits or losses. In corporate America you will find an alarming number of Type D organizations: International Harvester, Pan Am, Eastern Airlines, American Motors, Manville, U.S. Steel, National Steel, Warner Communications, Continental Illinois, Financial Corporation of America, Asarco, and Pabst Brewing, to name several. As we consider the ways in which this type of company can correct its problems, we'll examine some of these well-known companies in more detail—not in any presumptuous effort to tell them how to run their businesses, but in an effort to help you learn the precise steps you can take to overcome your problems and begin creating excellence.

HOW COMPANIES BECOME TYPE D ORGANIZATIONS

Before you can successfully move out of this category, you must understand how companies fall into it. Type D organizations usually exhibit three common attributes: imperceptiveness, defensiveness, and lack of consistency.

Imperceptiveness

Type D organizations seldom recognize the difference between a serious problem and a relatively minor one, a tendency that leads them to confront all problems or issues with the same level of two important resources—their people's working time and the company's money. Such imperceptiveness regarding the relative seriousness of problems paves the road to mediocrity. Several years ago the U.S. automobile industry continued to pay equal attention to all aspects of car-making but failed to perceive that fuel economy and car size were becoming primary issues. Consequently it didn't respond to these issues until foreign competitors shocked the industry into recognition. General Motors and Ford were large enough to absorb the consequences of their imperceptiveness, but Chrysler and American Motors experienced severe difficulties.

American Motors, formerly a Type D organization unable to marshal its resources to solve any one of its burdensome problems, racked up fourteen consecutive quarters of losses, but the company has hopefully begun to improve its situation, partly through its partnership with Renault, an alliance designed to resolve one of the company's most serious problems—product quality. The new compact Alliance automobile recently won distinction as *Motor Trend*'s Car of the Year. Chrysler, another once imperceptive automotive giant, began moving out of its own type D status when newly hired Lee Iaccoca immediately perceived cost reduction and new product development as the most serious problems the company had to solve.

Defensiveness

Type D organizations take defensive positions, reacting to crises rather than acting to prevent them in the first place. Such a stance is understandable because a company in trouble usually finds itself so beset with problems that it must spend all available energy and resources putting out present fires. Unfortunately, such a stance puts a company forever behind the crest of the wave of change.

East Asian and smaller domestic steel manufacturers have been segmenting steel markets in increasingly sophisticated ways for some time, but U.S. Steel, once a preeminent example of American industrial strength, continued to operate like a steel supermarket, offering all kinds of steel for all kinds of purposes. In its worst position in years, U.S. Steel reacted to its own near-collapse by acquiring Marathon Oil, paying $5.9 billion at a time when oil prices were at their peak. This reaction may or may not help the company's financial position, but it won't solve its steel-business problems. In contrast to U.S. Steel, National Steel has been aggressively attempting to exit Type D status by cutting its production capacity in half and slashing its work force from 27,000 to 11,000. But the company hasn't stopped there. It entered into a joint venture by selling half its steel operations to Japan's Nippon Kokan. Nippon Kokan, along with other Japanese steelmakers, has forged a leadership position by producing high-quality steel at lower costs than U.S. companies. Although National has bet its future on the joint-venture strategy with Nippon Kokan, it has also begun shoring up its culture by cutting back and regrouping.

Lack of Consistency

Type D organizations lack the strategic and cultural consistency that characterizes excellence. Their strategic directions shift and change spasmodically, and their corporate cultures suffer from incomprehensible alterations in underlying values and orientations.

Eastern Airline's CEO, Frank Borman, promised employees that wage concessions, amounting to 18 percent to 22 percent cuts in wages in return for company stock, would end December 31, 1984, but then he unilaterally attempted to extend the concessions into 1985. The result was traumatic. Three Eastern Airlines unions filed suits in two federal district courts challenging the move to extend the wage concessions. The real blow, however, was to the company's culture. One employee said the attempt to extend the concessions "reinforces the feeling that Eastern never keeps its word." Now the profit picture for 1985 appears dim. Another airline, Pan Am, has also languished as a Type D organization, having lost $762 million since 1980 and having suffered a strike at the beginning of 1985 that pushed the airline even closer to bankruptcy. The turmoil and unrest at Pan Am, although lessening, sprang from the company's

lack of a consistent winning strategy supported by a stable culture.

Since to some degree these three attributes usually infect an organization pursuing a bad strategy with a weak culture, you should learn to spot them before taking any corrective steps. Keeping an eye open for these attributes may help you avoid the Type D trap in the first place. If, however, you have classified your company as a Type D, you will want to contemplate the general sorts of actions you can take to improve your classification.

FIVE RULES OF THUMB FOR MANAGING TYPE D ORGANIZATIONS

Despite the increasing numbers of failures and bankruptcies, every year many companies, even the most seriously troubled, manage to turn things around. A study of such cases reveals five rules for getting out of the Type D predicament:

1. Know your relative position. Given the great diversity of organizations in the real world, a company's relative position inside the Type D category should help guide its course of corrective action. As you can see in the following example, a company with relatively more serious problems may move in a direction quite different than one with relatively less serious ones:

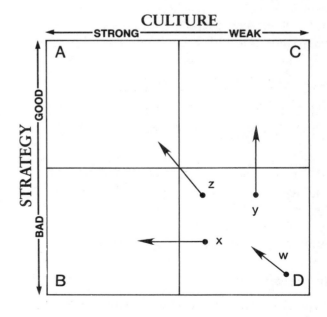

When Eastern Airline employees became stockholders, owning 25 percent of the company's stock in exchange for wage cuts, that event propelled the company near the "x" position. This would suggest that Eastern's first step on the road to recovery might be actions that would turn it into a Type B organization before it tries to go all the way to Type A. A strong culture characterizes Type B, and Eastern moved strongly in that direction with its employee ownership program. Unfortunately, Borman may have hindered further progress by attempting to extend the wage concessions into 1985 when he had promised otherwise. At a time when a strengthened culture could help Eastern, Borman's decision to favor a short-term strategic move over a longer-term culture-building effort may have moved the company closer to the "w" position in the grid. National Intergroup (National Steel) was pursuing a course from the "w" position as it cut costs and established two of the six lowest-cost mills in the U.S. Doubting the company's ability to make it into Type A status on its own, National's chairman Howard Love moved the company to a "y" position as he focused on a joint-venture arrangement that promised to solve the company's long-term strategy problems.

2. Avoid being overly ambitious. Unless your company's management team can successfully employ strategic thinking and corporate culture-building skills at the same time, you won't be able to move diagonally from Type D to Type A. Making a diagonal move requires a huge investment of time, money, and energy.

In one unusual case, Lee Iaccoca has undertaken this kind of transition at Chrysler. Whether the company will fully exit the Type D category and permanently enter the Type A category will not be clear for some time, but the company has moved in that direction. Iaccoca cut Chrysler's payroll in half and shut down one-third of the company's plants, thereby establishing the new basis for a high-productivity culture. At the same time, he strategically positioned the company for the future by investing in new product development that would eventually produce a string of successful cars. Although Iaccoca and his management team have accomplished the rare feat of simultaneously

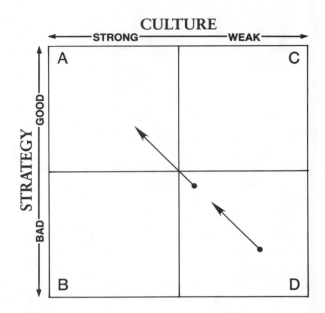

managing both strategy and culture, few organizations can hope to emulate such a move and should, instead, set their sights on improving from a Type D organization to Type C or B.

3. Move to Type C. Most Type D organizations find it more logical and practical to strive for Type C status by aggressively improving or changing market position through better strategies. As we have indicated, a company can more easily embark on a new strategic direction than on a cultural one. As you can see in the next chart, one company might work on its strategy without any attention to culture ("m"), while another might focus on strategy but take some small steps to improve culture at the same time ("n"). Depending on the course taken, a company could wind up in any number of relative positions inside the Type C quadrant.

To improve your strategy you can redesign it yourself, hire a strategy consulting firm, bring aboard new executives with the right kind of strategic experience, or merge with another company that already has a good strategy. American Motors combined several of these approaches to help lift it from Type D status. After greatly improving its market position through its partnership with Renault and the initial success of the Alliance, AMC also enhanced its own Jeep line and won numerous

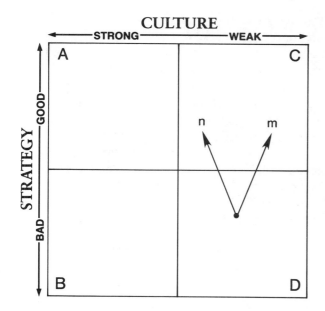

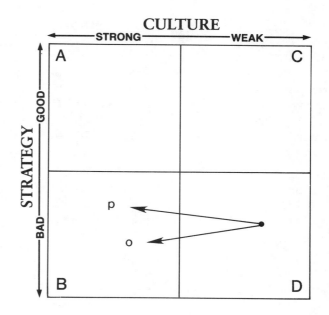

awards in 1984 for its new Jeep Cherokee. Despite the fact that the company must yet solve a host of culture problems, it has clearly used a successful strategy to progress toward Type C status.

Financial Corporation of America, the largest U.S. thrift institution, struggles with its Type D status by cutting back on its financial operations nationwide while at the same time slowly beginning to shore up its smaller, more manageable culture and tempering its innovativeness. FCA was simply moving too fast to manage its sprawling operations effectively— which led to its Type D status in the first place. Now, trying to get out means reversing the growth that had once been a rallying cry for the company.

4. Move to Type B. It takes even more skill to move a Type D organization into the Type B category by changing the corporate culture. In the following chart, the "o" company might work exclusively on its culture while the "p" company might add some strategic thinking to its preoccupation with improving its culture.

As with improvement to Type C status, when moving to Type B status you can try to rebuild your own culture, bring in a culture consultant, hire a superb culture-builder, or merge with a culture-rich corporation. In each case, you will want to proceed cautiously because all of these methods pose problems. Since your

management team functions as part of your own culture, it may lack sufficient objectivity to make crucial changes. Of course, even a new management team will have to work with the same employees. Replacing everyone is almost never feasible or wise. Finally, for many cultures, especially weak ones, a merger may create more confusion than it's worth.

If you feel you can afford the time, you should ideally reshape your company's culture from inside as McDonald Steel did. While U.S. Steel was trying to buy its way out of the steel business and its Type D status, McDonald's David Houck was reopening closed U.S. Steel mills and turning them into profitable businesses with a new culture. Houck, a steel mill supervisor for U.S. Steel, stayed in McDonald, Ohio, after his employer shut down the town's mill. Houck, determined to bring new life to the steel business, used venture capital to create a new business out of the old, establishing a corporate culture that eliminated the deadly attributes of U.S. Steel's culture: an overstaffed bureaucracy, a self-serving and political union, and widespread inefficiencies. Houck built the new culture with ex-union steelworkers, some of whose families had belonged to the union for generations but were eager to do whatever they had to do to save their livelihoods. The bureaucracy all but disappeared and efficiency increased dramatically as the workers, who share in the profits, took such innovative steps as working night shifts to take advantage of lower electric rates and scrounging up used equipment and parts at half the cost of new ones. It took three years, but McDonald Steel put over 100 people back to work and created hundreds of spin-off jobs in the community. Sales for 1984 reached $20 million, with earnings of $1 million; the company expects sales of $28 million in 1985. With a revitalized culture in place, David Houck has turned his attention to future strategies, such as considering the possibility of a full-blown minimill that could produce finished products from scratch. If Houck's strategies match his culture, McDonald Steel may someday enjoy Type A status.

Pabst Brewing has languished in Type D status for years and recently has had to fight off numerous takeover attempts. Today Pabst president William Smith is attempting to strengthen his company's culture by concentrating his attention on selling beer and at the same time searching for strategies that will improve the market positions of its products.

5. *Be persistent and patient.* Corporate comebacks take time and require an extreme amount of patience and persistence. Regardless of your relative position on the classification chart, and no matter which direction you plan to move, you cannot let the magnitude of the problem paralyze you. Taking no action will cause your situation to do nothing but deteriorate:

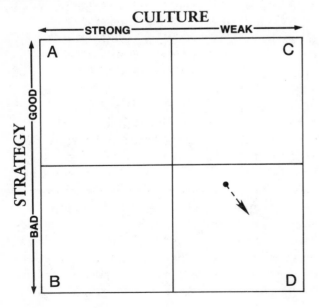

International Harvester, having exhibited Type D attributes for years, went through the motions of cutting costs and repositioning itself in the market, but close scrutiny reveals that the company did not really alter its poor strategic positions in numerous markets and that its fragmented culture stressed cost-cutting one day and better marketing the next. Without real progress toward a stronger culture or a better strategy, IH kept declining as its management failed to attack the roots of the company's problems. Today IH's new CEO, Donald Lennox, claims to be making real progress on both fronts, but it will take him years to raise the company from its deteriorated Type D status.

ACTION PLANS

With the three Type D attributes and the five rules of thumb in mind, you can begin to shape your own action plans. As you engage in the following three exercises, you will be turning your insights from Chapter 7 into specific actions that may set you on the road to recovery. First you will design preliminary action plans, then you will test those plans with the Strategy-Culture Matching Grid before finalizing the changes you should make.

EXERCISE 1
DEVELOPING PRELIMINARY ACTION PLANS

By the end of Part A of this exercise, you should have determined your basic direction. Will you set your sights on becoming a Type C organization by changing your strategy? Will you aim at Type B status by changing your culture? Or will you try to move into Type A by attacking both at once? In Part B of the exercise you will begin listing specific actions you might take to embark on your chosen path. But before you begin, review your evaluation of current strategy and culture and your scenarios for change in Chapter 7.

As we have seen, American Motors took the strategy path, trying to better satisfy customer needs with a reliable and economical new car that could compete effectively against the Japanese imports. AMC combined its own strength with that of its partner, Renault. McDonald Steel chose the culture route, building commitment among employees to help turn a profit in a tough business. Competence emerged and the company perpetuated both the commitment and competence by recruiting ex-union employees who would perform any job necessary for a company that cared as much about them as they cared about the company. Iacocca chose the strategy-culture route, paying attention to all six strategy-culture factors simultaneously.

Whichever course you select on the basis of your relative position in the classification chart and your intimate knowledge of your own organization, you should begin by describing proposed changes and restating your strategy or culture in light of those changes. Keep all six strategy-culture components in mind, basing your statements on the overall conclusions and future directions you developed in Chapters 1–6 and summarized in Chapter 7. In Part B of this exercise you will list specific steps your company might take in the first through the fifth years of its change implementation program. Steps for the first year should be extremely specific, while longer-range steps can be more general.

Let's go back to our national discount chain from Chapter 2. As you saw in the Introduction to Part II, the discount chain graded itself 15 on culture and 21 on strategy, thus putting itself in the Type D category. Because the discount chain falls closer to Type C than Type B status on the chart, the company decided to put all its energies behind strategy, boosting it beyond its B− rating. The company filled out Part A of Exercise 1 as follows (note that no changes in culture were contemplated for the time being).

EXERCISE 1 EXAMPLE, PART A

---

1. Strategy

A. **Proposed changes in the way your company satisfies customer needs:** *Emphasize meeting customers' financing needs through a wide range of new financial services.*

B. **Proposed changes in the way your company sustains competitive advantage:** *Stay 3 to 5 years ahead of our competitors in terms of the breadth, convenience, and cost of our financial services.*

C. **Proposed changes in the way your company capitalizes on company strengths:** *Build on credit-card financing strengths by offering additional specialized financial services to our best credit card customers.*

Restatement of your company's overall strategy: *Maintain customer loyalty through existing merchandising practices with a new emphasis on financial services that will make it increasingly easier and preferable to do business with us.*

As you proceed with this exercise, you will want to fill out *all* the sections. Although you may end up focusing on either strategy or culture over the short term, you will have to tackle both over the long haul.

EXERCISE 1 WORKSHEET PART A

Developing Preliminary Action Plans

1. Strategy

A. Proposed changes in the way your company satisfies customer needs: _____
_____
_____
_____
_____
_____

B. Proposed changes in the way your company sustains competitive advantage: _____
_____
_____
_____
_____
_____
_____
_____

C. Proposed changes in the way your company capitalizes on company strengths: _____
_____
_____
_____
_____
_____
_____
_____

Restatement of your company's overall strategy: _____
_____
_____
_____
_____
_____
_____

2. Culture

D. Proposed changes in the way your company cultivates commitment to the company's common purpose: _____
_____
_____
_____
_____
_____

E. Proposed changes in the way your company develops competence to deliver superior performance: _____
_____
_____
_____
_____
_____

F. Proposed changes in the way your company maintains consistency in perpetuating commitment and competence: _____
_____
_____
_____
_____
_____

Redefinition of your company's culture: _____
_____
_____
_____
_____
_____

When the national discount chain executives considered specific actions they might take, they completed the first-year section for Part B like this:

EXERCISE 1 EXAMPLE, PART B

1. Strategy

A. Steps to implement changes in the way we satisfy customer needs:

First year:
Survey credit card holders to identify interest in alternative financial services.

Select financial services of greatest interest and develop implementation schedules.

Introduce a minimum of two new financial services to all customers this year.

B. Steps to implement changes in the way we sustain competitive advantage:

First year:
Institute a semiannual competitor review process to identify what new financial services are being offered.

Develop relationships with a local bank to handle selected financial services.

Sell corporate headquarters on a company-wide strategy to increase and enhance financial services.

C. Steps to implement changes in the way we capitalize on company strengths:

First year:
Solidify the loyalty of our most preferred and active credit card holders by offering one new special financial service.

Move more customers into the preferred customer ranks by reducing the interest charge when monthly purchases reach an established minimum.

Again, you will want to fill out all sections of this exercise, regardless of whether you will be working to improve either strategy or culture in the near future.

EXERCISE 1 WORKSHEET PART B

Developing Preliminary Action Plans

1. Strategy

A. Steps to implement changes in the way we satisfy customer needs:

First year: _____

_____

_____

_____

_____

Second and third years: _____

_____

_____

_____

_____

Fourth and fifth years: _____

_____

_____

_____

_____

B. Steps to implement changes in the way we sustain competitive advantage:

First year: _____

_____

_____

_____

Second and third years: _____

_____

_____

_____

Fourth and fifth years: _____

_____

_____

_____

_____

_____

C. Steps to implement changes in the way we capitalize on company strengths:

First year: _____

_____

_____

_____

_____

Second and third years: _____

_____

_____

_____

_____

Fourth and fifth years: _____

_____

_____

_____

_____

_____

2. Culture _____

_____

_____

_____

_____

D. Steps to implement changes in the way we cultivate a commitment to a common purpose:

First year: _____

_____

_____

_____
_____
_____

Second and third years: _____
_____
_____
_____
_____

Fourth and fifth years: _____
_____
_____
_____
_____

E. **Steps to implement changes in the way we develop competence to deliver superior performance:**

First year: _____
_____
_____
_____
_____
_____

Second and third years: _____
_____
_____
_____
_____

Fourth and fifth years: _____
_____
_____
_____
_____

F. **Steps to implement changes in the way we consistently perpetuate commitment and competence:**

First year: _____
_____

_____
_____
_____
_____

Second and third years: _____
_____
_____
_____
_____
_____

Fourth and fifth years: _____
_____
_____
_____
_____

EXERCISE 2
TESTING YOUR PLANS WITH THE STRATEGY-CULTURE MATCHING GRID

Before you refine your plans for action, you should run each proposed change through the Strategy-Culture Matching Grid, rating all the different combinations of strategy-culture components as excellent, good, fair, poor, or bad in terms of their matches. If you have grown proficient with the grid, you can perform this exercise mentally. Remember, you should run your changes through the grid one at a time. Whether you are contemplating changes in all six factors or just one, we recommend you walk through each affected match one at a time, weighing all possible consequences.

When the national discount chain applied the matching grid to its proposed changes in strategy, it reached some interesting insights. One of these was the mismatch between the company's proposed action to stay three to five years ahead of competitors in the area of financial services. Here executives found a major mismatch between this element of strategy and the company's dominant merchandising competence (see the example on the facing page).

CULTURE

D. _____
_____

E. *Merchandising Know-how*

F. _____
_____

STRATEGY

A. _____
_____
_____

1.	*2.*	*3.*
4.	*5. Matching Grade:* _D_	*6.*
7.	*8.*	*9.*

B. **Stay 3 to 5 Years Ahead of Competitors in Financial Services**

C. _____
_____
_____

Evaluation of Match

5. Match between B and E

Grade   _D_

Rationale:
The company's strategy to stay ahead of competitors in terms of financial services does not draw on the company's traditional dominant competence.

Testing Your Plans with the Strategy-Culture Matching Grid

CULTURE

D. _____   E. _____   F. _____

STRATEGY

A. _____

B. _____

C. _____

	D.	E.	F.
A.	1. Matching Grade: _____	2. Matching Grade: _____	3. Matching Grade: _____
B.	4. Matching Grade: _____	5. Matching Grade: _____	6. Matching Grade: _____
C.	7. Matching Grade: _____	8. Matching Grade: _____	9. Matching Grade: _____

Evaluation of Match

1. Match between A and D:

Grade _____   Rationale: _____

_____

_____

_____

2. Match between A and E:

Grade _____   Rationale: _____

_____

_____

_____

3. Match between A and F:

Grade _____   Rationale: _____

_____

_____

_____

4. Match between B and D:

Grade _____   Rationale: _____

_____

_____

_____

5. Match between B and E:

Grade _____   Rationale: _____

_____

_____

_____

6. Match between B and F:

Grade _____   Rationale: _____

_____

_____

_____

7. Match between C and D:

Grade _____   Rationale: _____

_____

_____

_____

8. Match between C and E:

          Grade _____   Rationale: _____
_____
_____
_____

9. Match between C and F:

          Grade _____   Rationale: _____
_____
_____
_____

EXERCISE 3
FINALIZING YOUR PLANS

If you have thoroughly tested all relevant matches, you can now refine the steps you will take to effect changes in strategy and/or culture. If you identified unacceptable mismatches in Exercise 2, you will undoubtedly want to fine-tune your plans in light of them.

Remember, you eventually want to orchestrate strategy and culture in harmony. In the short term you may wisely choose to tolerate a mismatch between a strategy component and a culture component, but the long-term list of actions should include an eventual effort to bring the match into line. For example, when Iaccoca cut Chrysler's payroll in half and invested heavily in new product development, that action sent a shock wave through the culture; but after the culture absorbed the shock, Chrysler's innovative, market-driven strategy gave rise to a streamlined efficient, productivity-oriented culture.

After completing Exercise 2, the national discount chain wondered whether its new strategic emphasis on financial services would really work. The executives recognized that the chain served many metropolitan areas around the country, and that unless the parent embraced the new strategy the mismatch between culture and strategy would prevent them from staying three to five years ahead of competitors. Knowing the entrenched nature of the company's culture, particularly in the area of the chain's dominant merchandising competence, they asked themselves whether the corporate culture could really change sufficiently over time to allow the chain to retain a leading edge in financial services. They filled out the strategy portion of Part A of Exercise 3 as follows.

EXERCISE 3 EXAMPLE, PART A

1. Strategy

A. **Final changes in the way your company satisfies customer needs:** *No change.*

B. **Final changes in the way your company sustains competitive advantage:** *In order to stay 3 to 5 years ahead of competitors in the area of customer financial services, we must acquire these capabilities through merger or some kind of joint venture with a financial services company at the national level.*

C. **Final changes in the way your company capitalizes on its strengths:** *No change.*

Final statement: *Maintain our retail customers' loyalty by continuing to enhance and improve current merchandising practices while at the same time entering into a merger or cooperative arrangement with a financial services company at the national level in order to offer an increasingly broad range of financial services designed to make it more convenient, inexpensive, and enjoyable for customers to do business with us.*

EXERCISE 3 WORKSHEET PART A

Finalizing Your Plans

1. Strategy

A. Final changes in the way your company satisfies customer needs: _____
_____
_____
_____
_____
_____
_____

B. Final changes in the way your company sustains competitive advantage: _____
_____
_____
_____
_____
_____
_____
_____
_____

C. Final changes in the way your company capitalizes on its strengths: _____
_____
_____
_____
_____
_____
_____
_____

Final statement of your company's strategy: _
_____
_____
_____
_____
_____
_____
_____
_____

2. Culture

D. Final changes in the way your company cultivates commitment to its common purpose: _____
_____
_____
_____
_____
_____
_____
_____

E. Final changes in the way your company develops competence to deliver superior performance: _____
_____
_____
_____
_____
_____

F. Final changes in the way your company maintains consistency in perpetuating commitment and competence: _____
_____
_____
_____
_____
_____
_____

Final definition of your company's culture: _
_____
_____
_____
_____
_____
_____
_____
_____

In Part B, the national discount chain executives had to take into account that the four stores in question represented only a part of the entire company and therefore concluded that long-term implementation of their strategy depended on the entire company pursuing the same strategy; otherwise their ability to stay ahead of competitors would decrease over the next few years.

EXERCISE 3 EXAMPLE, PART B

1. Strategy

A. **Final steps to implement changes related to satisfying customers:** *On hold until corporate headquarters provides guidance.*

B. **Final steps to implement changes related to sustaining competitive advantage:**

   First year: *Report findings and recommendations of our extensive strategy-culture assessment to the national office and request guidance for next steps.*

C. **Final steps to implement changes related to capitalizing on company strengths:** *On hold until corporate headquarters provides guidance.*

Fortunately, the discount chain's headquarters did give the task force guidance to move ahead, saying "do all you can to offer new financial services in your own market over the next one to two years." By that time headquarters expected to have worked out an arrangement to establish some form of "family bank" in every store across the nation. It took the task force six months of discussion and analysis but, as it turned out, its efforts provided the stimulus for the chain's decision to acquire the competence it needed to effectively carry out the proposed strategy.

EXERCISE 3 WORKSHEET PART B

Finalizing Your Plans

1. Strategy

A. Final steps to implement changes related to satisfying customers:

First year: _____

_____
_____
_____
_____
_____

Second and third years: _____

_____
_____
_____
_____
_____

Fourth and fifth years: _____

_____
_____
_____
_____
_____
_____
_____

B. Final steps to implement changes related to sustaining competitive advantage:

First year: _____

_____
_____
_____
_____

Second and third years: _____

_____
_____
_____
_____
_____
_____
_____
_____

Fourth and fifth years: _____

_____
_____
_____
_____
_____

C. Final steps to implement changes related to capitalizing on company strengths:

First year: _____

_____
_____
_____
_____

Second and third years: _____

_____
_____
_____
_____
_____

Fourth and fifth years: _____

_____
_____
_____

2. Culture

D. Final steps to implement changes related to cultivating commitment of a common purpose:

First year: _____

_____
_____
_____
_____

Second and third years: _____

_____
_____
_____
_____

Fourth and fifth years: _____
_____
_____
_____
_____
_____
_____

E. **Final steps to implement changes related to developing competence to deliver superior performance:**

First year: _____
_____
_____
_____
_____
_____

Second and third years: _____
_____
_____
_____
_____
_____

Fourth and fifth years: _____
_____
_____
_____
_____
_____
_____

F. **Final steps to implement changes related to maintaining consistency in perpetuating commitment and competence:**

First year: _____
_____
_____
_____
_____
_____

Second and third years: _____
_____
_____
_____
_____
_____
_____

Fourth and fifth years: _____
_____
_____
_____
_____
_____

CONCLUSION

You should now have in hand a document you can use to guide your pursuit of excellence. Like many other problems in our society, admitting the problem in the first place presents the biggest hurdle. Being a troubled company should not embarrass or anger you but stimulate you to take charge of your destiny. Every year companies get into trouble with their strategies and cultures, and every year some flee to the bankruptcy courts—but many others stage impressive comebacks. You too can bail yourself out of your difficulties if you admit your problems, fully assess their causes, and take decisive action.

As you embark on your program of change, try to keep all the lessons of this book in mind, but, first and foremost, emphasize the positive new direction you're taking and school yourself in the art of patience.

CHAPTER 9

TYPE C ORGANIZATIONS

Type C organizations have adopted excellent strategies but have not yet nurtured the strong corporate cultures they need to consistently implement them. Many such companies have so squarely set their sights on short-term success that they practically worship strategy and pay scant attention to developing the sort of culture needed for long-term success. Although a Type C organization may enjoy a string of short-term triumphs by following strategies that stress acquisitions, new markets, or new products, their weak, underdeveloped corporate cultures inevitably halt their march toward excellence. A few well-known Type C companies are Apple, Commodore, Compaq, ITT, RCA, Dart & Kraft, Sears, B. F. Goodrich, and Allegheny International. All embarked on brilliant strategies that won them initial successes but then found themselves in difficulty as their weak cultures began to struggle.

HOW COMPANIES BECOME TYPE C ORGANIZATIONS

Type C organizations invariably display three common attributes. Only after you have learned to recognize and understand these attributes can you hope to move your own company out of the Type C category.

Overadaptation to Opportunities

Type C organizations tend to be obsessed with adapting to change. While adapting to change should preoccupy the execupreneur, overstressing adaptation usually causes a company to become opportunistic in the extreme, constantly shifting strategies without sufficient regard for the company's culture. RCA, once the pioneer of the electronics industry, lost its edge in electronics through inattention to its cultural trait of technological supremacy and began weaving a tapestry of uncoordinated acquisitions and strategic directions under five different CEOs. The acquisitions, ranging from car rental to publishing to financial services to frozen foods, seemed to guarantee a bright future and short-term boosts in financial performance. Each seemed poised to grasp the "hot" industry of the day. However, RCA's series of opportunistic and overly adaptive strategic moves left the company's culture in a shambles, fragmented and confused. By letting the flurry of strategies and acquisitions overshadow the ever-weakening culture, RCA found itself sinking to the ranks of the least-admired companies in America.

By the same token, Sears, anxious to build on its base of 52 million credit card customers, its nationwide network of stores, and its Allstate insurance business, also fell victim to overadaptiveness when it leaped into the stock brokerage and real estate businesses by buying Dean Witter and Coldwell Banker. Then, thirsting for even more change, the company entered a host of new businesses, including dental offices, car rental services, optical shops, and, a new possibility, "family banks." Although Sears has managed these new endeavors better than most companies could, we believe it has crossed over the line from Type A into Type C status. No matter how brilliant its strategy, its culture cannot possibly absorb so much change without a great deal of anguish. Last year's losses by Dean Witter and the continuing strain of adapting to change have confused and weakened the Sears culture to the point that future excellence depends on Sears' ability to concentrate on fully integrating all its businesses. Otherwise it will drift further into Type C status.

Obsession with Growth

Type C organizations often overemphasize growth, either using it to maintain their market share in an expanding industry or simply to satisfy a desire for empire building. These companies suffer from a common American illusion that "bigger is better," a preoccupation that can cause a company to become greedy, always breaking new ground before shoring up the ground that has already been taken. Harold Geneen built ITT into an empire by adhering to a strategy based on acquisition and financial control. By constantly acquiring companies, then placing strict financial requirements upon them, Geneen racked up an impressive annual growth record for some fifteen years. Under his direction the company grew from $766 million to $22 billion. Growth in sales and earnings dominated ITT until Geneen's retirement. When the new CEO, Rand Araskog, decided he had to get the company's culture to concentrate more on the common purpose of running the advanced technology businesses that had made ITT a dominant force abroad, he began lopping off businesses ill-suited to that purpose. ITT's growth strategy had created a far-flung empire with a diverse sub-culture, that only Harold Geneen could hold together. Araskog backed off on growth strategies to focus instead on nurturing a commitment and competence in telecommunications. Continuing Geneen's growth strategy was really not an option for Araskog if he expected to create excellence because it was becoming more and more difficult for anyone, other than Geneen, to manage the multitude of businesses that composed ITT by the late 1970's. Such diversity and fragmentation with nothing more than sales growth and profit objectives as a common bond do not lend themselves to the development of a strong, integrated corporate culture, particularly after the organization's architect and builder steps down as CEO.

Dart & Kraft offers another enlightening example of the perils of short-term growth strategies. Before he died, Justin Dart, who had been obsessed with growth his entire career, merged his $2.5-billion Dart Industries with Kraft Foods to create the crowning jewel of his empire, but the empire began crumbling as the merged culture wallowed without clear direction. Was the new company a food company, a consumer goods manufacturer, a marketing company, an aggressive acquirer of other companies, or just a hodgepodge conglomerate? No one seemed to know for sure. Fortunately, today Dart & Kraft has returned to the basics, trying to strengthen the internal cultures of its major businesses and figure out what fits and what doesn't—the only steps the company can take to rid itself of the burdens of a Type C organization.

Orientation Toward Disposable Cultures

A Type C organization usually embraces strategy so completely that it tends to see its culture as an element of corporate life it can easily throw away and replace. Such shortsightedness eventually does great damage, because a culture's central asset is its people, and they will not sacrifice themselves for ever-changing, task-oriented strategies. At Commodore, Jack Tramiel earned a reputation as an executive who never built a permanent organization. All he seemed to care about were strategy and results. To be sure, his strategies worked, helping Commodore sell over a million home computers in 1982 and beat that record in the last three months of 1983 alone, thus driving Texas Instruments, Mattel, and Timex out of the market. In 1984 the company surpassed $1 billion in sales and $100 million in profits. During his tenure, however, Tramiel employed a rash of presidents, hired and fired countless advertising agencies and marketing personnel, and terminated independent sales representatives in favor of the company's own sales force, only to disband the group three months later. Under his administration, the only permanent fixture at Commodore was Jack Tramiel himself, and he ruthlessly pursued but one goal—increasing Commodore's market share—no matter how many people it burned up. Toward the end of Tramiel's tenure at Commodore, before he left for Atari, the company's reputation was making it difficult to attract good, qualified people. Unless Commodore begins building for the long term by giving its people a greater sense of permanency, it will not be able to hire and retain the people it needs to create excellence or even stay in business. The disposable-culture approach has worked for Commodore in the past, but as the word gets around, potential recruits, unwilling to be viewed as disposable, will avoid the company.

Apple Computer has sinned somewhat less in this regard. Striving to retain a technological edge, Apple has forced its culture to take a back seat to strategy, isolating the Macintosh team from the rest of the company to protect its integrity. The hiring of John Sculley to inject some professional management into Apple underscored the fact that the company was suffering a cultural identity crisis. Can Sculley unify the Apple culture around the sort of commitment and competence that made the Macintosh a success? If so, Apple may quickly rise above Type C status. However, the most disturbing thing about Apple Computer is the transition it is attempting to make from entrepreneurial innovator to professional marketer. It is attempting to do both, but can it continue? Will Apple sacrifice its innovative culture with all its intellectual freedom and stimulating camaraderie, or will it sacrifice the marketing prowess that Sculley is trying to solidify? Must one of these cultures be disposed of, or can Apple serve both masters, innovation and marketing? And what about the effect of merging the company's nine highly decentralized divisions into one centralized organization? Who is Apple, really? Part of that question was answered when Steve Jobs, cofounder and chairman of Apple, was stripped of all operating authority and subsequently resigned a few months later. Now other questions arise: What will Apple become under Sculley's sole leadership. Can Apple make it into Type A status or will it drift into a Type D status?

FIVE RULES OF THUMB FOR MANAGING TYPE C ORGANIZATIONS

If you find yourself in a Type C predicament, you should observe the five rules of thumb for improving your situation.

1. Find your company's relative position. Your specific course of action will depend on your relative position inside the Type C quadrant. From point "x" or "w" (see following diagram) you can probably enter Type A status directly, while from point "z" you would most likely pass through Type B before reaching Type A. Finally, since point "y" lies just a short step from Type D, this position requires extreme caution. As the grid illustrates, Type C companies usually move along curved paths, not the straight ones we saw for Type D organizations. The curved paths represent the fact that shifting focus from strategy to culture usually weakens strategy in the short term because culture building requires such a concentration of effort and resources that it tends to distract an organization from its short-term strategy moves.

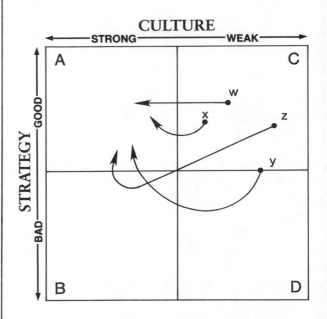

Apple might now lie close to point "x," while Commodore undoubtedly lies closer to point "z." Apple can probably go directly to Type A status by continuing to define and emphasize its corporate culture, constantly articulating its values and bringing more consistency to its internal environment. On the other hand, Commodore's strategy will surely suffer if and when the company attacks its "disposable" culture problem because it will no longer be able to scrap an existing culture to pursue a hot new strategy.

2. Move to Type A. Despite the difficulties involved, moving directly to Type A makes sense for a lot of firms. However, doing so requires a lot of experience and skill at simultaneously managing strategy and culture. Even with a particularly strong strategy in place, you will often find that concentration on strengthening culture weakens strategy over the short haul. Company "m" illustrates this phenomenon. Most executives and organizations can't maintain a heavy emphasis on strategy when they begin shoring up their culture. Still, assuming the prerequisite skills, a direct move, as taken by company "n," can save time and energy:

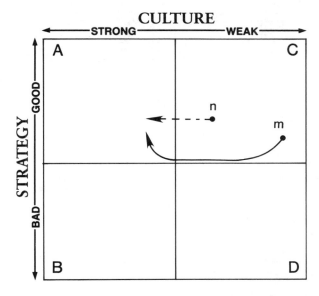

Sears has attempted to skillfully balance its strategy and culture and seems to be making this type of move. Although the company's aggressive growth strategy did inflict a degree of chaos on the organization, thereby weakening the corporate culture, Sears nevertheless has striven to build a new culture to match its new strategy. It has placed Dean Witter and Coldwell Banker departments inside Sears stores in an effort to integrate the entire family of services and products. And special training for store and department managers has helped employees to understand and embrace the company's new posture. Only time will tell whether Sears' move back into Type A status will resemble an "n" or an "m" company.

3. Move to Type B. If you determine that increased attention to your culture will initially weaken your strategy, thereby forcing you through Type B status before you can reach Type A, you should not resist such a delayed route. Culture building takes time and money, and strengthening a weak culture demands an extraordinary investment. At the same time, the typical Type C organization often finds it necessary to greatly reduce its overemphasis on strategy, an undertaking that can halt any string of short-range strategic successes. Although carefully and patiently building your company's culture to match your strategy may force you to delay fully implementing your strategic direction, do not abandon your strategy but keep your eye on an eventual transition to Type A:

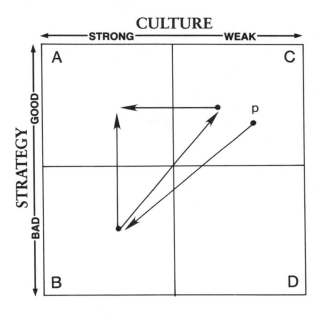

ITT finds itself in a situation similar to company "p." Araskog's decision to build a technologically advanced telecommunications company while divesting the company of some of the results of Geneen's aggressive strategic moves may have propelled ITT on a path from Type C to Type B, but Araskog certainly has set his long-range sights on Type A. However, if ITT remains Type B for too many years, it may have to go back through Type C before entering Type A (as illustrated by company "p" above) because an emphasis on strategy usually weakens culture in the short term, and an emphasis on culture usually weakens strategy in the short term. Staying a Type B company too long may require an inordinate emphasis on strategy again to move into Type A status. Fortunately, ITT may find a move to Type A easier then because it will be in a relatively stronger Type C position.

RCA, too, has been divesting itself of poorly fitting businesses and has halted the succession of acquisitions in favor of trying to figure out what the company is really all about. If it establishes clear commitment, competence, and consistency, it may make a smooth progression through Type B to Type A status.

4. Remain temporarily at Type C. While some companies can pursue a string of short-term strategies for quite a few years, as ITT's Harold Geneen proved, and still others can continue to frequently redefine their cultures for quite a while, as Commodore's Tramiel proved, the history of corporate failures suggests that no organization can do so forever. At some point a company's ability to maintain a string of strategies declines as it exhausts the culture's best efforts, and the culture responds less and less well to what it sees as unstable or insensitive leaders. In such a situation both strategy and culture can eventually decline.

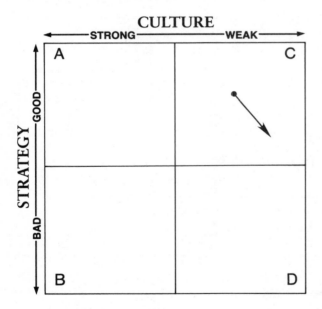

Commodore International got away with cultural inconsistencies for a long time because Jack Tramiel's street-fighting strategies could plow under all competitors, and the company was always able to attract people with battling mentalities. However, with Tramiel gone to Atari, Commodore's reputation as a company that chews people up and spits them out has

worsened and the days of the disposable culture have come to a crashing stop. If Commodore does not take action, it may soon decline into Type D.

5. Build your culture with deep sensitivity. Regardless of the direction you decide to take, you should immediately find ways to improve your culture. Your success depends on adopting a long-range perspective and addressing your people's needs with an abiding and honest caring. Without such action you will eventually slide into Type D status:

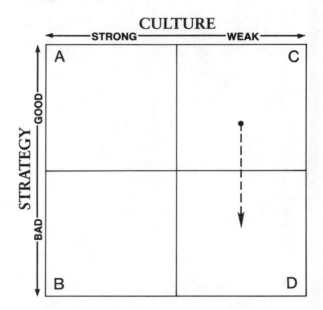

When the dust settled after the Dart-Kraft merger, it became painfully clear to the company's executives that they had to bolster their fragmented, unfocused culture or suffer dire consequences. It took a lot of sensitivity for Dart & Kraft to begin building its businesses from the inside out instead of through acquisitions.

Keep these rules of thumb in mind as you consider your own course of action for improving your Type C situation. You can continue to buy, hire, or develop new strategies that will mask the ills of your weak corporate culture, and you may even stay close to the leading edge of innovation in your industry, but unless you focus on culture building at some point your situation will most certainly become worse.

ACTION PLANS

Keeping in mind the attributes of Type C organizations and the specific changes you contemplated in Chapter 7, you can now begin to take action. In the following three exercises you will first formulate preliminary action plans for changing your culture and, given the changes, for modifying your strategy correspondingly; then you will use the Strategy-Culture Matching Grid to test the effects of proposed changes before finalizing them.

EXERCISE 1
DEVELOPING PRELIMINARY ACTION PLANS

In Part A of this exercise you will summarize proposed changes in the three culture components and, as a consequence of those changes, make any necessary adjustments to the three strategy factors. The sweeping changes undertaken by most Type C organizations in their approach to culture building almost always force some changes in their strategic directions. Once you have isolated all potential changes, you should restate your company's strategy and culture to encompass those changes.

In Part B, you will begin to detail specific steps for strengthening your culture.

Remember JCN from Chapter 4? The company defined its common purpose as: "Knowledgeably deliver the most innovative and advanced computer technology to technically sophisticated customers, thereby supporting our customers' own innovations and providing our people with the satisfaction and financial rewards of enhancing our customers' accomplishments." You may recall that top management was committed to this mission but the R&D department, probably the most important group in the company, was not. If you turn back to the Introduction to Part II, you will see that JCN rated its strategy 33 out of a possible 36 and its culture 21 out of a possible 36. The company's strategy had attained success and profit but it had also masked the company's underdeveloped culture. JCN filled out the Culture section of Exercise 1, Part A, this way:

EXERCISE 1 EXAMPLE, PART A

---

1. Culture

A. **Proposed changes in the way your company cultivates commitment to a common purpose:** *We must communicate our company's purpose and strategy much more completely and consistently to all R&D personnel, thereby increasing understanding* *of the company's purpose and encouraging input and feedback. Once our R&D people understand the company's purpose and strategy, we must enter into an ongoing dialogue to achieve their buy-in.*

B. **Proposed changes in the way your company cultivates competence to deliver superior performance:** *Our dominant competence is and must remain applied research in the areas of technically sophisticated, engineering-oriented computer hardware and software. Currently that research is not sufficiently focused to keep us on the leading edge in our markets. The focus of our research must be narrowed and more productive.*

C. **Proposed changes in the way your company maintains consistency in perpetuating commitment and competence:** *While we have consistently stressed R&D as the most critical function in our culture, we must pay more attention to the commitment of our research scientists to our common purpose, and to their focus on R&D competence.*

   Redescribe your company's culture incorporating the above changes: *Our company's culture must become a combination of the above statements. Our R&D people must be committed to and competent in delivering the most technically advanced computer applications to technically sophisticated customers.*

Regardless of the factors you anticipate changing, try to fill in each section of this exercise.

EXERCISE 1 WORKSHEET, PART A

Developing Preliminary Action Plans

1. Culture

A. Proposed changes in the way your company cultivates commitment to a common purpose: _____

_____

_____

_____

_____

_____

B. Proposed changes in the way your company cultivates competence to deliver superior performance: _____

_____

_____

_____

_____

_____

C. Proposed changes in the way your company maintains consistency in perpetuating commitment and competence: _____

_____

_____

_____

_____

_____

Redescribe your company's culture incorporating the above changes: _____

_____

_____

_____

_____

_____

_____

_____

2. Strategy

A. Modifications in the way your company satisfies customer needs: _____

_____

_____

_____

_____

_____

_____

B. Modifications in the way your company sustains competitive advantage: _____

_____

_____

_____

_____

_____

C. Modifications in the way your company capitalizes on company strengths: _____

_____

_____

_____

_____

Restate your company's strategy incorporating the above modifications: _____

_____

_____

_____

_____

_____

_____

_____

JCN filled out the Culture section of Part B in the following manner:

EXERCISE 1 EXAMPLE, PART B

---

1. Culture

A. Steps to implement changes in the way you cultivate commitment to a common purpose:

First year:
Develop a brief company document describing top management's desired common purpose and all that it implies.

Distribute documents to R&D personnel and ask for specific feedback.

Conduct a series of discussions with key R&D people to ensure understanding of the common purpose and to mold, if necessary, that purpose to lay the foundation for commitment.

Second and third years:
Establish a monthly dialogue session with key research scientists to discuss ways to increase commitment to the common purpose.

Help research scientists who cannot buy in to find employment options elsewhere.

Redesign the company's hiring practices to increase screening of candidates in an effort to improve the likelihood of genuine buy-in to the common purpose.

Fourth and fifth years:
Terminate any of the original research scientists that have still not bought in. Make sure they have adequate employment options elsewhere before termination.

Again, fill out each section, even if you do not plan an immediate change in that area.

EXERCISE 1 WORKSHEET, PART B

1. Culture

A. Steps to implement changes in the way you cultivate commitment to a common purpose:

First year: _____
_____
_____
_____
_____

Second and third years: _____
_____
_____
_____
_____
_____

Fourth and fifth years: _____
_____
_____
_____
_____

B. Steps to implement changes in the way you develop competence to deliver superior performance:

First year: _____
_____
_____
_____
_____

Second and third years: _____
_____
_____
_____
_____

Fourth and fifth years: _____
_____
_____

_____
_____
_____
_____

C. Steps to implement changes in the way you maintain consistency in perpetuating commitment and competence:

First year: _____
_____
_____
_____
_____

Second and third years: _____
_____
_____
_____
_____

Fourth and fifth years: _____
_____
_____
_____
_____

2. Strategy

A. Modifications in the way your company satisfied customer needs:

First year: _____
_____
_____
_____

Second and third years: _____
_____
_____
_____
_____

EXERCISE 1 WORKSHEET, PART B (*Cont.*)

Fourth and fifth years: _____
_____
_____
_____
_____
_____

B. Modifications in the way your company sustains competitive advantage:

First year: _____
_____
_____
_____
_____
_____
_____

Second and third years: _____
_____
_____
_____
_____
_____
_____

Fourth and fifth years: _____
_____
_____
_____
_____
_____

C. Modifications in the way your company capitalizes on company strengths:

First year: _____
_____
_____
_____
_____
_____

Second and third years: _____
_____
_____
_____
_____
_____

Fourth and fifth years: _____
_____
_____
_____
_____
_____

EXERCISE 2
APPLYING THE STRATEGY-CULTURE MATCHING GRID

In this exercise you will use the Strategy-Culture Matching Grid to assess the effects of each proposed change on each of the other strategy-culture components. Although you will spend most of your time weighing the nine combinations that result from your new culture-building plan, you will also run any strategy adjustments through their nine combinations. As before, you will rate each combination with a rating from A+ to F. Once you have rated a particular combination, be sure to record the rationale behind it.

When the JCN executives used the Strategy-Culture Matching Grid to test impact on strategy and culture of proposed changes in culture and minor modifications in strategy, they felt quite confident because the match seemed nearly perfect on paper. To illustrate why the JCN executives felt so elated, consider one of their nine matches, shown in the following example.

CULTURE

D. Deliver the Most
Innovative and
Technically Advanced
Computer
Technology to
Technically   E. _____   F. _____
Sophisticated   _____   _____
Customers   _____   _____

STRATEGY

A. **Offer Products**
   that Meet
   Sophisticated
   Customers'
   Needs for State-
   of-the-Art
   Computer
   Hardware and
   Software

1. *Matching Grade:*	2.	3.
A		
4.	5.	6.
7.	8.	9.

B. _____
   _____
   _____

C. _____
   _____
   _____

Evaluation of Match

1. Match between A and D:

Grade   *A*   **Rationale:**
*The company's methods of satisfying
customer needs perfectly matches the
common purpose and needed commitment.*

    Bear in mind that you may want to test matches, make adjustments, then test them again. The matching grid should be a dynamic tool, not one you use once and then discard as you make changes in your organization.

Applying the Strategy-Culture Matching Grid

CULTURE

D. _____ E. _____ F. _____

STRATEGY

A. _____

1. Matching Grade: ___	*2. Matching Grade:* ___	*3. Matching Grade:* ___
4. Matching Grade: ___	*5. Matching Grade:* ___	*6. Matching Grade:* ___
7. Matching Grade: ___	*8. Matching Grade:* ___	*9. Matching Grade:* ___

B. _____

C. _____

Evaluation of Match

1. Match between A and D:

Grade _____   Rationale: _____

_____

_____

_____

2. Match between A and E:

Grade _____   Rationale: _____
                         _____
                         _____
                         _____

3. Match between A and F:

Grade _____   Rationale: _____
                         _____
                         _____
                         _____

4. Match between B and D:

Grade _____   Rationale: _____
                         _____
                         _____
                         _____

5. Match between B and E:

Grade _____   Rationale: _____
                         _____
                         _____
                         _____

6. Match between B and F:

Grade _____   Rationale: _____
                         _____
                         _____
                         _____

7. Match between C and D:

Grade _____   Rationale: _____
                         _____
                         _____
                         _____

EXERCISE 2 WORKSHEET (*Cont.*)

8. Match between C and E:

Grade _____   Rationale: _____
_____
_____
_____

9. Match between C and F:

Grade _____   Rationale: _____
_____
_____
_____

EXERCISE 3
FINALIZING ACTION PLANS

Now you should be able to finalize your course of action. In light of insights gained from Exercise 2, modify your preliminary changes and action plans accordingly. Because JCN's test with the matching grid uncovered no mismatches or problems, the company's preliminary plans became its final plans. Nevertheless, JCN's executives recognized that after ongoing discussion sessions with research scientists they might need to make some modifications to their plans, slightly altering either strategy or culture, then again applying the matching grid to determine congruence. In fact, nine months after embarking on their plans to change their culture, they did make some changes. After numerous sessions with key R&D personnel, the company decided to broaden its purpose and strategy by once again attacking additional markets where the need for technically advanced hardware and software was emerging. You can see in the following example how the JCN executives used Exercise 3, nine months after the first run-through, to modify one element of its strategy in support of a broadened mission statement.

EXERCISE 3 EXAMPLE, PART A

1. Strategy

A. **Final changes in the way your company satisfies customer needs:** *We will satisfy customers in the same way, but we will seek out an ever expanding base of customer segments.*

EXERCISE 3 EXAMPLE, PART B

1. Strategy

A. **Final steps to implement changes related to satisfying customer needs:**

First Year:
Commission a leading market research firm to identify additional market segments needing our technically advanced computer products now or in the future.

Determine priority of each new segment and develop marketing plan for entry into the top three market segments.

Initiate entry into one of the top three market segments.

Second and third years:
Initiate entry into the next two market segments.

Conduct additional market research to find additional market segments.

Develop marketing plans for promising segments.

Fourth and fifth years:
Continue expanding the application of technically advanced computing hardware and software.

As the computer company's executives did, you may want to repeat this exercise six to twelve months after you have inaugurated any changes.

EXERCISE 3 WORKSHEET, PART A

Finalizing Your Plans

1. Strategy

A. Final changes in the way your company satisfies customer needs: _____

_____

_____

_____

_____

_____

B. Final changes in the way your company sustains competitive advantage: _____

_____

_____

_____

_____

_____

C. Final changes in the way your company capitalizes on company strengths: _____

_____

_____

_____

_____

_____

Final statement of your company's strategy in terms of capitalizing on company strengths: _

_____

_____

_____

_____

_____

_____

_____

2. Culture

D. Final changes in the way your company cultivates commitment to its common purpose: _____

_____

_____

_____

_____

_____

E. Final changes in the way your company develops competence to deliver superior performance: _____

_____

_____

_____

_____

F. Final changes in the way your company maintains consistency in perpetuating commitment and competence: _____

_____

_____

_____

_____

_____

Final definition of your company's culture in terms of consistency in perpetuating commitment and competence: _____

_____

_____

_____

_____

_____

_____

_____

EXERCISE 3 WORKSHEET, PART B

Finalizing Action Plans

1. Strategy

A. **Final steps to implement changes related to satisfying customer needs:**

First year: _____

_____

_____

_____

_____

_____

_____

Second and third years: _____

_____

_____

_____

_____

_____

_____

Fourth and fifth years: _____

_____

_____

_____

_____

_____

_____

_____

B. **Final steps to implement changes related to sustaining competitive advantage:**

First year: _____

_____

_____

_____

_____

Second and third years: _____

_____

_____

_____

_____

_____

_____

Fourth and fifth years: _____

_____

_____

_____

_____

_____

_____

C. **Final steps to implement changes related to capitalizing on company's strengths:**

First year: _____

_____

_____

_____

_____

_____

Second and third years: _____

_____

_____

_____

_____

_____

Fourth and fifth years: _____

_____

_____

_____

_____

_____

2. Culture

D. **Final steps to implement changes related to cultivating commitment to a common purpose:**

First year: _____

_____

_____

_____

_____

EXERCISE 3 WORKSHEET, PART B (*Cont.*)

Second and third years: _____

_____
_____
_____
_____

Fourth and fifth years: _____

_____
_____
_____
_____

E. **Final steps to implement changes related to developing competence to deliver superior performance:**

First year: _____

_____
_____
_____
_____

Second and third years: _____

_____
_____
_____
_____

Fourth and fifth years: _____

_____
_____
_____
_____

F. **Final steps to implement changes related to maintaining consistency to perpetuating commitment and competence:**

First year: _____

_____
_____

_____
_____
_____
_____
_____

Second and third years: _____

_____
_____
_____
_____

Fourth and fifth years: _____

_____
_____
_____
_____

When JCN modified both its strategy and culture as a result of valuable input from the research scientists, it used the matching grid to further refine all elements of its strategy and culture. For example, the grid helped JCN determine that an improved strategy, applying leading-edge technology to an ever-expanding customer base, would require dual competence, coupling the company's R&D competence with a market application competence over the long term.

CONCLUSION

If you make successful adjustments to your corporate culture, you should find your company moving steadily, if slowly, into the Type B or Type A category. In the next two chapters we will learn how to move from Type B to Type A, then we will consider the ways in which the Type A organization works diligently to maintain its excellence.

CHAPTER 10

TYPE B ORGANIZATIONS

Type B organizations display strong corporate cultures but have not yet marshaled them behind brilliant strategies. Many such companies once enjoyed Type A status with strong cultures and excellent strategies, but as external conditions changed they did not evolve their strategies to successfully fulfill the needs of the marketplace. Consequently, their corporate cultures could not productively direct their commitment and competence. If such a situation persists, the culture will eventually weaken, thus pulling the organization into Type D status. When strong cultures can't adapt to change or when a strategy ineffectively exploits the characteristics of a strong culture, one of the great tragedies in business occurs: a strong corporate culture, which took years of sensitivity and patience to cultivate, begins to deteriorate. A few well-known Type B companies are Procter & Gamble, Digital Equipment Corporation, General Motors, Johnson & Johnson, Merrill Lynch, Campbell Soup, Wang Laboratories, U-Haul, General Mills, Exxon, and Xerox. Let's look more closely at how some of these companies got themselves into trouble.

HOW COMPANIES BECOME TYPE B ORGANIZATIONS

Since three attributes generally characterize the Type B organization, recognizing and understanding them will help you deal with your own Type B status. Your insight should stimulate you to get your company back on the Type A track.

Resistance to Change

Type B organizations, believing that their strong cultures can conquer all obstacles, tend to resist change. These organizations don't deal adroitly with change because they have relied for so long on a profitable way of doing business that they blindly continue that approach. Of course, this inertia is understandable, given the time and effort it takes to remold a corporate culture. If a culture's consistency with respect to commitment and competence has figured prominently in any historical successes, management worries about upsetting the culture by redirecting it behind new strategies. Unfortunately, such fears can cause the leadership of a company to embrace a weakened strategy long after it made sense to develop alternatives.

Merrill Lynch enjoys an enviably strong corporate culture based on a painstakingly developed retail system of 431 branch offices and 8,763 brokers. As the financial services industry has undergone dramatic changes in recent years, Merrill Lynch has tried to move in new directions but has done so with poor strategies. While the company has attempted to develop and implement innovative strategies, it has not succeeded in delivering its expanded services and products to customers because its prices have not been competitive against lower-cost suppliers of similar services. Merrill Lynch's recent strategies have been the product of a slow-to-change culture and consequently have not been good enough to gain adequate penetration in new financial service markets. The company's traditional broker-dependent culture has attempted to develop fast-paced, quick-penetration strategies, but the strategies have not succeeded partly because Merrill Lynch's culture hasn't developed enough strategic insight and versatility over the years (when sameness and stability were most important) to launch successful strategies in a rapidly changing environment. The company's culture is strong, but its resistance to change has made it difficult for Merrill Lynch to develop competitively effective strategies. Its brokers' ingrained cultural traits make it hard for them to think of Sears Roebuck and others as bonafide competitors. The company's chairman, Roger Birk, hopes to redirect its strategy while at the same time adjusting the company's culture without destroying it. If he succeeds, he'll almost surely return Merrill Lynch to Type A status.

Xerox still seems destined to fall victim to its own resistance to change. Xerox, somewhat smug about the fact that people call almost any brand of copier a "Xerox," failed to employ a strategy that would sustain its early dominance, and upstarts such as Savin, Ricoh, Sharp, and Canon have taken big bites out of the market. While Xerox has long boasted a vigorous culture, it still hasn't found the strategies behind which its culture can successfully rally. Recently the company announced plans to close its Shugard Corporation disk-drive operations, marking yet another failure to maneuver in the modern high-tech world. Although Xerox can claim many important breakthroughs in technology, including the first personal computer, the company has consistently failed to turn those breakthroughs into best-selling products, because in most cases it lacked the right strategies to do so.

Blind Perpetuation of Tradition

Culture-rich, strategy-deficient organizations spend an inordinate amount of time and money perpetuating their strong cultures. When a company invests heavily in finding ways to do better what it already does well, it's called "entrenchment." These companies' strategies often fail because their tradition-bound cultures can't effectively implement them or because the strategies failed to adequately address the needs of the market in the first place. Procter & Gamble has experienced a decade of lackluster growth and in 1984 its earnings fell for the first time in thirty-three years. Although P&G deserves admiration for its culture's disciplined

marketing prowess, it receives lower marks for its strategic thinking. Some of the company's leading products, such as Pampers, Ivory, Tide, Cheer, Downy, and Crest, have been losing market share recently to smaller, more aggressive and nimble competitors who have beaten P&G to the marketplace. P&G's very strength, marketing thoroughness, has produced strategies that overemphasize comprehensive market testing, rejection of imitative products, abhorrence of the low-price segment of the market, and strict limitation of product-line extensions. Unfortunately, these old tried-and-true strategies have not fared well in a rapidly changing and increasingly competitive arena. While P&G perpetuates its once-reliable culture, it continues to lose ground in the marketplace. However, P&G has embarked on some cultural shifts by reducing market testing, pushing selected imitative products, developing some bargain brands, and extending numerous product lines. By bolstering and refining its strategy, P&G appears to be successfully staging a comeback to Type A status. But it's a delicate balance. If the company changes too much too soon, it could remain in Type B or find itself overcorrecting its problems and declining into Type C, with improved strategies but a weakened culture.

General Motors has also mortgaged its future by perpetuating its past. Assuming that the American public would continue to buy whatever Detroit produced, it got clobbered by foreign imports in the 1970s, as Japan's market share soared from 6 percent in 1971 to 21 percent in 1980. GM had perpetuated its consistent approach to making automobiles for so long that its culture simply couldn't respond fast enough to new trends like smaller cars, standardized options, and European design. Once-brilliant strategies soured into bad strategies. When the auto giant tried to regain market share by spending more than Ford, Chrysler, and AMC in the stampede toward more fuel-efficient, smaller cars, that strategy faltered too. Now, GM's new attention to a diversification strategy may help it profitably apply its strong culture.

Insufficient Strategic Thinking

Shallow strategic thinking frequently afflicts companies that don't look deeply enough for ways to reapply their already strong culture to a strategy that exploits the commitment, competence, and consistency of that culture. If a Type B organization grasps at an obvious strategy that promises to meet the changing needs of the marketplace and then expects a strong culture to easily adapt to that strategy, it usually finds the strategy failing because the culture can't implement it quickly or efficiently enough. Of course, the new strategy may be one that a refined culture should be able to handle, but it may also have been ill-conceived from the beginning. The astute managers of a Type B organization should spend a great deal of time contemplating a strong culture's strengths before launching strategies that apply those strengths. General Mills, well known for its strong food-marketing culture, failed to think through its entrance into the apparel and toy business and blithely expected its strong culture to handle almost any new business. However, since food-marketing prowess does not guarantee apparel- or toy-marketing success, General Mills' new ventures never paid off. In fact, it has put three of these businesses—Izod, Parker Brothers, and Kenner—up for sale and has returned to what it does best. If the company avoids strategies that conflict with its culture, it may once again rise to Type A status. Another food company, Campbell Soup, employed a similarly bad strategy when it tried to diversify away from foods. Happily, a new CEO, knowing that a strong culture is too valuable an asset to discard for a glamorous new strategy, has abandoned that strategy in favor of expanding into new food products.

FIVE RULES OF THUMB FOR MANAGING TYPE B ORGANIZATIONS

Execupreneurs can follow five rules of thumb for managing Type B organizations:

1. Find your company's relative position. Your remedial action will depend on your relative position inside the Type B quadrant. If your company lies at point "x" you can probably enter Type A status directly. If it lies at point "z" you will probably have to pass through the Type

C quadrant before entering A. Companies that sit at point "y" may find themselves moving temporarily through Type D status, so they must take great care that they don't get mired there but progress instead toward C and then A. Although it often makes sense to pursue a course similar to the one illustrated by point "w," most organizations do in fact take a roundabout route to Type A status because managing strategy and culture simultaneously can be such a difficult task.

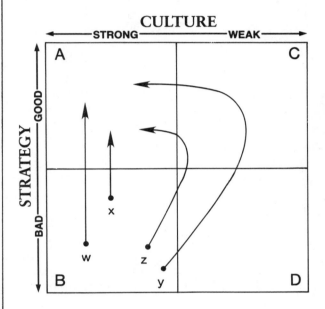

A company like Procter & Gamble probably occupies a point near "x" and can reenter Type A status as soon as its culture can implement its bolstered strategy. By contrast, a company like Xerox, having eroded some of the strength of its culture over the years as its strategies failed to work may be closer to point "y." It could be difficult for Xerox to take a direct route into Type A status because beefing up strategy may further encroach on the company's culture, while shoring up its culture would simply keep it a Type B.

2. Set your sights on Type A. Although most executives would prefer a direct move from Type B to Type A, few companies actually take that path because doing so requires careful and skillful attention to both strategy and culture. If you have determined that your company is a Type B, then you must develop a strategy that will successfully satisfy customer needs, sustain a competitive advantage, and capitalize on company strengths without running completely contrary to your culture's existing commitment, competence, and consistency. A strong culture can change to embrace a new strategy, but such change never happens overnight, and it takes a huge investment of time and energy.

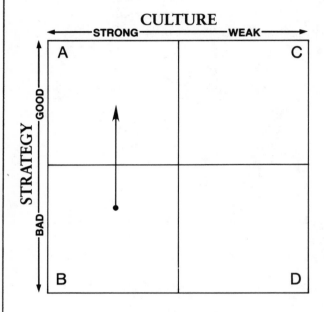

Although Merrill Lynch hopes to slip directly back into Type A status, the company's success in doing so will depend on whether or not its retail network of branches and brokers can comfortably adapt to the one-stop financial services strategy. The road back could be arduous and expensive, and it will certainly require a careful balancing of cultural changes with strategic decisions. The traditional broker mentality can't incorporate too much change too quickly, but the strategy can't be delayed so long that competitors claim all the new territory.

Procter & Gamble should encounter a less rocky road on its way to Type A status because it already sits so close to the border. Even though the company has undertaken drastic changes in its marketing strategy, the changes draw upon the company's historical marketing prowess. Still, though the company's commitment, competence, and consistency will remain fairly stable, P&G's major modifications in where and how to direct its marketing expertise will make it vital to monitor developments closely.

3. Move to Type C. Sometimes you cannot choose any course but a move from B to C. If your company's culture has weakened, pushing you to the brink of Type D status, and you have pursued all viable options for applying your culture in new ways, then you will undoubtedly move to a Type C organization. If so, you will be betting your future on a new strategy and hoping you can adjust your culture fast enough to make it work. Some companies in this position acquire other companies that offer some degree of the needed strategy and culture elements, but such a tactic can cause additional problems related to the integration of two different companies as the entities merge. Other companies hire consultants to design a new strategy, but consultants seldom have the skills for concurrently reshaping a client's culture. Only a company's own people can do that. Sadly, some companies wait until their strong culture has deteriorated to the point where salvaging it will take as much effort as building a new one from scratch.

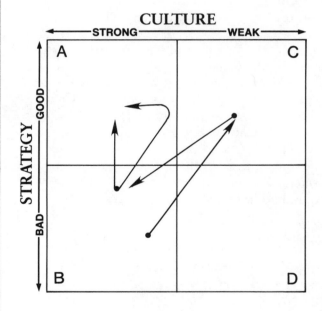

Both Campbell Soup and General Mills took an excursion into Type C as they renounced their strong cultures and embraced new strategies. Fortunately, both these companies realized the folly of compromising culture for the sake of an expedient strategy and both have managed themselves back to Type B status, from where they can try to move directly into A. Their brief forays into Type C status taught them painful but instructive lessons. Johnson & Johnson, in its bid to gain leadership in the high-tech medical field, has recently pushed part of its organization into Type C. The new strategy could brilliantly win a market niche in future medical technology, but the change has hurt J&J's strong culture and as a result has lost millions of dollars. J&J seems committed to making the change by building a new kind of J&J culture behind the new strategy, but success lies some distance in the future. Such a bold departure from the company's strong culture may be the only way for J&J to change creatively, but it will pay a high price for any eventual success.

4. Stay in Type B, but not forever. Strong cultures don't die easily; they can limp behind a poor strategy for many years. In fact, when a culture is in need of adaptation to change the best thing to do may be to let it languish for a while until people inside the organization see the need for change and are willing to move.

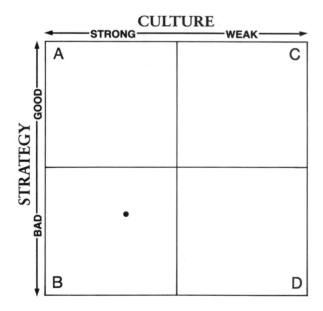

In a classic case of this sort of behavior, General Motors lived with a bad strategy for several years before responding to the threat of foreign competition, but through it all remained one of the largest companies in the world and improved its strategy while still remaining a Type B organization. The stronger the culture, the longer a company can survive with an ailing strategy. Strong cultures usually enjoy long enough histories of accumulated successes that people working in such situations master the confidence and commitment to make the best of what they have to work with. Digital Equipment Corporation's position began declining quickly when the advent of the microcomputer derailed the company's minicomputer strategy, forcing DEC to scramble into an office systems and networking strategy to avoid serious damage. However, DEC cannot survive its Type B status for very long without incurring a great deal of cultural damage because DEC's culture lacks the accumulated history that GM enjoyed and is more vulnerable to poor strategies. Before you decide to stay in Type B status, make sure you fully understand your culture's ability to withstand the inevitable blows it will receive.

5. Strategically apply your culture with deep insight. Inaction will invariably push your company into Type D status because a bad strategy will eventually destroy a culture, no matter how strong it has been in the past.

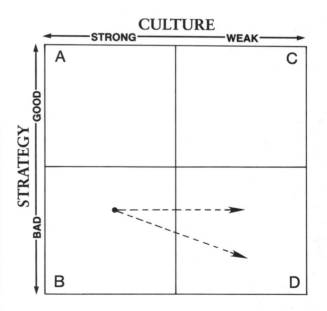

In order to avoid drifting into Type D status you must take some kind of strategic action that will not run completely counter to the nature and abilities of your strong culture. Remember, you want to find the right strategy with limited and acceptable implications for your people. Focus your attention on future strategies that take into account the essence of your company's culture and that will take fullest advantage of it as you chart a new course. Exxon did this wisely when it stopped looking for diversification opportunities such as office systems businesses and narrowed its focus to oil exploration and production, finding new ways to grow by applying its strong oil-oriented culture. General Mills also moved in a smart direction when it stopped taking its food-marketing culture too far afield into other businesses and started implementing insightful food-marketing strategies that could take advantage of the company's strong culture.

Keep these rules of thumb in mind as you consider your own course from Type B to Type A status. You can buy, hire, or develop new strategies that look marvelous on paper, but if your culture can't successfully unite behind one of these brilliant strategies, you haven't made any progress on the road to excellence. Type B organizations should constantly seek creative ways to apply their cultures in new ways, in new markets, and with new strategies. A strong culture will serve a company better in the long run than a strong strategy without a matching culture or a string of strategies that keep the culture fragmented and off-balance.

ACTION PLANS

Keeping in mind how companies become Type B and the rules of thumb for managing Type B organizations, you can now begin constructing action plans. In the following three exercises, you will again move from preliminary plans based upon proposed changes in strategy and/or culture, through application of the Strategy-Culture Matching Grid, and at last to finalization of your plans.

EXERCISE 1
DEVELOPING PRELIMINARY ACTION PLANS

In this exercise you will record each of the changes in strategy and/or culture you identified in Chapter 7. Part A will include all potential changes in each of the six strategy and culture components, and in Part B you will sketch your proposals for implementing those changes. Procter & Gamble identified large changes in its strategy that required some slight modifications in the application of its culture. The new strategic direction helped P&G develop and get its products to market faster, which required the culture to become less cautious. When General Motors concluded that outspending other domestic carmakers wouldn't stop foreign manufacturers from making inroads, it developed action plans to diversify and acquired Ross Perot's Electronic Data Systems and then Hughes Aircraft.

You'll recall the Landon Corporation example from Chapter 1, which presented a sign company attempting to better understand its customers and improve its strategies. Phil Landon filled out Part A of Exercise 1 in the following way.

1. Strategy

A. Proposed changes in the way your company satisfies customer needs: *Our customers need much more assistance in determining the primary purpose of the signs they use than we have provided. We must improve our ability to provide that assistance.*

B. Proposed changes in the way your company sustains competitive advantage: *Becoming the best consulting firm for signs, as well as producing high-quality signs, will give us a substantial long-term advantage in our industry.*

C. Proposed changes in the way your company capitalizes on company strengths: *We need to capitalize on our superior understanding of the uses and purposes of signs.*

Restatement of your company's overall strategy: *Our strategy is to not only produce the highest quality signs possible, but to make sure that every customer gets the right sign for the right purpose.*

Fill out every section of this exercise, even if you do not contemplate a change in that area at the moment.

Developing Preliminary Action Plans

1. Strategy

A. Proposed changes in the way your company satisfies customer needs: _____

_____

_____

_____

_____

_____

_____

B. Proposed changes in the way your company sustains competitive advantage: _____

_____

_____

_____

_____

_____

_____

_____

C. Proposed changes in the way your company capitalizes on company strengths: _____

_____

_____

_____

_____

_____

_____

Restate your company's strategy incorporating the above changes: _____

_____

_____

_____

_____

_____

_____

2. Culture

A. Modifications in the way your company cultivates commitment to a common purpose: _____

_____

_____

_____

_____

_____

_____

_____

B. Modifications in the way your company develops competence to deliver superior performance: _____

_____

_____

_____

_____

_____

_____

_____

C. Modifications in the way your company maintains consistency in perpetuating commitment and competence: _____

_____

_____

_____

_____

_____

_____

Redescribe your company's culture incorporating the above modifications: _____

_____

_____

_____

_____

_____

_____

Phil Landon filled out the first section of Part B as follows:

EXERCISE 1 EXAMPLE, PART B

1. Strategy

A. **Steps to implement changes in the way you satisfy customer needs:**

First year:
Develop a corporate brochure on the purpose of signs.

Establish a set of procedures for assisting customers in determining the primary purpose of a proposed sign prior to writing an order.

Set a company policy that no orders for signs be accepted without an explicit statement of the intended purpose of the sign, written by Landon Corp. engineers after consultation with the customer.

Second and third years:
Create a videotape presentation that walks customers through a comprehensive yet brief explanation of the many purposes of signs, highlighting the major mistakes most customers make when selecting a sign, even when they have the benefit of their advertising agency's input.

Establish a 3-month training program for new employees that will enable them to provide consulting assistance to customers.

Fourth and fifth years:
Update brochures, video presentations, policies, and training courses as needed.

Again, do this exercise in its entirety.

EXERCISE 1 WORKSHEET, PART B

Developing Preliminary Action Plans

1. Strategy

A. Steps to implement changes in the way you satisfy customer needs:

First year: _____
_____
_____
_____
_____
_____

Second and third years: _____
_____
_____
_____
_____
_____

Fourth and fifth years: _____
_____
_____
_____
_____
_____

B. Steps to implement changes in the way you sustain competitive advantage:

First year: _____
_____
_____
_____
_____
_____

Second and third years: _____
_____
_____
_____
_____
_____

Fourth and fifth years: _____
_____
_____
_____
_____
_____
_____
_____

C. Steps to implement changes in the way you capitalize on company strengths:

First year: _____
_____
_____
_____
_____

Second and third years: _____
_____
_____
_____
_____

Fourth and fifth years: _____
_____
_____
_____
_____
_____

2. Culture

A. Steps to implement modifications in the way you cultivate commitment to a common purpose:

First year: _____
_____
_____
_____
_____

Second and third years: _____
_____
_____
_____
_____
_____
_____

Fourth and fifth years: _____
_____
_____
_____
_____
_____
_____

B. Steps to implement modifications in the way you develop competence to deliver superior performance:

First year: _____
_____
_____
_____
_____
_____
_____
_____

Second and third years: _____
_____
_____
_____
_____
_____
_____

Fourth and fifth years: _____
_____
_____
_____
_____
_____
_____

C. Steps to implement modifications in the way you maintain consistency in perpetuating commitment and competence:

First year: _____
_____
_____

_____
_____
_____

Second and third years: _____
_____
_____
_____
_____
_____
_____

Fourth and fifth years: _____
_____
_____
_____
_____
_____
_____
_____
_____

EXERCISE 2
APPLYING THE STRATEGY-CULTURE MATCHING GRID

At this point you again want to rate the matches between each of the nine strategy-culture combinations as excellent, good, fair, poor, or bad. If you use the grid creatively, you will be able to thoroughly test the congruence between your strategy and culture in light of anticipated changes identified in Exercise 1. If Campbell Soup and General Mills had employed such a test prior to their diversifying out of foods, they might have avoided the problems they encountered and begun pursuing their current strategies much sooner.

When Phil Landon tested his new strategy with the grid, he found some mismatches he would have to correct. For example, the company's existing culture was not geared toward ample communication with customers about the primary purpose of their signs. The following is an example of the kind of mismatch Landon found.

CULTURE

D. _____

E. Engineering and Production Expertise That Produces the Best-Quality Signs in the Northwest

F. _____

STRATEGY

A. Assist Customers in Determining Primary Purpose of Their Signs Before Producing the Highest-Quality Signs Possible

1.	2. Matching Grade: ___C+___	3.
4.	5.	6.
7.	8.	9.

B. _____

C. _____

Evaluation of Match

2. Match between A and E:

Grade ___C+___

Rationale: *The competence to produce a superior-quality sign does not ensure effective communication with customers regarding the primary purpose of their signs.*

Applying the Strategy-Culture Matching Grid

CULTURE

D. _____

E. _____

F. _____

STRATEGY

A. _____

1. Matching Grade: _____	*2. Matching Grade:* _____	*3. Matching Grade:* _____
4. Matching Grade: _____	*5. Matching Grade:* _____	*6. Matching Grade:* _____
7. Matching Grade: _____	*8. Matching Grade:* _____	*9. Matching Grade:* _____

B. _____

C. _____

Evaluation of Match

1. Match between A and D:

Grade _____   Rationale: _____

_____

_____

2. Match between A and E:

            Grade _____   Rationale: _____
_____
_____
_____

3. Match between A and F:

            Grade _____   Rationale: _____
_____
_____
_____

4. Match between B and D:

            Grade _____   Rationale: _____
_____
_____
_____

5. Match between B and E:

            Grade _____   Rationale: _____
_____
_____
_____

6. Match between B and F:

            Grade _____   Rationale: _____
_____
_____
_____

7. Match between C and D:

            Grade _____   Rationale: _____
_____
_____
_____

EXERCISE 2 WORKSHEET (*Cont.*)

8. Match between C and E:

Grade _____

Rationale: _____
_____
_____
_____

9. Match between C and F:

Grade _____

Rationale _____
_____
_____
_____

EXERCISE 3
FINALIZING ACTION PLANS

In this exercise you will outline your company's final action plans in light of alterations dictated by your use of the grid. As you make these modifications you may want to repeat Exercise 2 several times, testing any new matches. In Part A you will record your final action plans with respect to each of the changes you intend making in either your strategy or your culture. Then in Part B you will record a final summary of your company's strategy and culture. This final statement should satisfy all the requirements of a successful strategy and a strong culture, as well as exhibit a harmonious match between them.

When it came time for Phil Landon to finalize his strategy and culture, he made no significant changes in strategy beyond those proposed in Exercise 1. However, after applying the matching grid, he did decide to slightly adjust his corporate culture. He filled out a portion of Parts A and B of Exercise 3 in the following way.

EXERCISE 3 WORKSHEET, PART A

Finalizing Your Plans

1. Strategy

A. Final changes in the way your company
satisfies customer needs: _____
_____
_____
_____
_____
_____
_____
_____
_____

B. Final changes in the way your company
sustains competitive advantage: _____
_____
_____
_____
_____
_____
_____
_____
_____
_____

C. Final changes in the way your company
capitalizes on company strengths: _____
_____
_____
_____
_____
_____
_____
_____

Final statement of your company's strategy in
terms of capitalizing on company strengths: _
_____
_____
_____
_____
_____
_____
_____
_____
_____

2. Culture

D. Final changes in the way your company
cultivates commitment to its common
purpose: _____
_____
_____
_____
_____
_____
_____
_____

E. Final changes in the way your company
develops competence to deliver
superior performance: _____
_____
_____
_____
_____
_____

F. Final changes in the way your company
maintains consistency in perpetuating
commitment and competence: _____
_____
_____
_____
_____
_____
_____

Final definition of your company's culture in
terms of consistency in perpetuating
commitment and competence: _____
_____
_____
_____
_____
_____
_____
_____

EXERCISE 3 WORKSHEET, PART B

Finalizing Action Plans

1. Strategy

A. Final steps to implement changes related to satisfying customer:

First year: _____
_____
_____
_____
_____
_____

Second and third years: _____
_____
_____
_____
_____
_____

Fourth and fifth years: _____
_____
_____
_____
_____
_____

B. Final steps to implement changes related to sustaining competitive advantage:

First year: _____
_____
_____
_____
_____

Second and third years: _____
_____
_____
_____
_____

Fourth and fifth years: _____
_____
_____
_____
_____
_____

C. Final steps to implement changes related to capitalizing on company strengths:

First year: _____
_____
_____
_____
_____
_____

Second and third years: _____
_____
_____
_____
_____
_____

Fourth and fifth years: _____
_____
_____
_____
_____

2. Culture

D. Final steps to implement changes related to cultivating commitment of a common purpose:

First year: _____
_____
_____
_____

Second and third years: _____
_____

EXERCISE 3 WORKSHEET, PART B (*Cont.*)

_____
_____
_____

Fourth and fifth years: _____

_____
_____
_____
_____

E. **Final steps to implement changes related to developing competence to deliver superior performance:**

First year: _____

_____
_____
_____
_____

Second and third years: _____

_____
_____
_____
_____

Fourth and fifth years: _____

_____
_____
_____
_____

F. **Final steps to implement changes related to maintaining consistency in perpetuating commitment and competence:**

First year: _____

_____
_____
_____
_____
_____

Second and third years: _____

_____
_____
_____
_____
_____

Fourth and fifth years: _____

_____
_____
_____
_____

CONCLUSION

Type B organizatins come closer to excellence than Type C or D because they enjoy the valuable and hard-won asset of a strong culture. Next we will examine the best of all possible worlds—the Type A organizations that have all the assets needed to establish excellence. Surprisingly, managing such companies requires no less skill and diligence than managing the turnarounds we discussed earlier.

CHAPTER 11

TYPE A ORGANIZATIONS

Every company strives for the ideal embodied in the Type A organization. Not only do excellent firms enjoy strong cultures and successful strategies, but they also forge a superb match between the two. Some organizations have remained Type A for years, while others have resided there only briefly because their leaders lacked the perennial skills needed to keep them there. If the ideal takes time and effort to achieve, maintaining it takes even more. A few well-known Type A companies are IBM, General Electric, Dow Jones, American Express, Marriott, Coca-Cola, 3M, Merck, Hewlett-Packard, Delta Air Lines, Citicorp, Hallmark, Eastman Kodak, Dayton Hudson, and Boeing. Although some enjoy secure Type A positions, others hold a precarious grip on theirs. Nevertheless, they all provide instructive models.

HOW COMPANIES BECOME TYPE A ORGANIZATIONS

Type A organizations display three common attributes. Recognizing and understanding these attributes will enable you not only to develop them in your own company but to perpetuate them far into the future.

Using Insightful Strategies to Seize Opportunities

The executives who run Type A companies bring terrific insight to their strategic thinking as they astutely search for better ways to satisfy customers, sustain their advantage over competitors, and capitalize on company strengths. One of the best of these companies, General Electric, claims that over 75 percent of its managers are masterful strategic thinkers or have at least taken strong steps in that direction. Seventy-five percent may seem high until you realize that the company has been promoting strategic planning and management for the past twenty years, and so strategic thinking and the resultant insight have become second nature for most GE managers. When Jack Welch, the company's CEO, laid out his vision of the future ("Every business will be a leader in its market or hold a technological advantage"), the company's managers responded with enough strategic insight to turn the dream into a reality.

Coca-Cola, another Type A organization, also displayed great strategic insight when it engineered the landmark success of diet Coke. No soft drink in recent history has won such an immediate and large market share. However, the company's latest decision to alter its 100-year-old formula for Coca-Cola, and then to reintroduce the old formula as Coke "Classic," may or may not represent the same kind of insight. No matter what the final verdict, you can count on Coca-Cola to keep thinking of new ways to try to outwit Pepsi.

Remaining Sensitive to Cultural Characteristics

Type A organizations pay tremendous attention to their cultures, handling them with the utmost care and sensitivity. That doesn't mean the executives in such firms behave in an overly cautious or soft-hearted fashion, but it does mean they highly value their people and their collective commitment, competence, and consistency. The way IBM takes care of its sales force, the people who are closest to the company's customers, illustrates the company's extreme sensitivity to maintaining its "superior customer service" culture. Such cultural sensitivity leads to the sort of meticulous attention to detail and special touches you see at IBM sales meetings. IBM executives take great pains with such meetings, flying their sales people to exotic locations, then pampering them and motivating them with professionally polished presentations and performances (always world-class events), inspiring film profiles of consistently outstanding sales people, black-tie banquets, and a host of other events that make IBM's sales people feel like royalty. Why does the company spend so much time and money to create that feeling? Because it enriches and enhances IBM's most prized possession: its corporate culture.

Citicorp, too, enriches its culture by infusing into every person in the organization the innovative and versatile spirit of former CEO Walter Wriston. As a result, Citicorp attracts a different breed of manager, one committed to action, innovation, and risk taking. John Reed, Wriston's hand-picked successor, perfectly fits the Wriston mold and has bet heavily on the bank's credit card business, the same way Wriston bet on financial service offices in every state in the Union, thus skirting interstate banking laws. Can Reed manage Citicorp's culture with Wriston's consummate skill? If he can, Citicorp's Type A position will remain secure for many years to come.

Maintaining a Balanced Strategy-Culture Alloy

Type A organizations make sure strategy and culture components always match. Managers of Type A companies that retain their enviable status possess such a deeply ingrained, almost intuitive sense of who they are and where they're going that they usually avoid the tangents and detours that can dissolve the strategy-culture alloy. In the midst of criticism, management changes, and market shifts, 3M and Hewlett-Packard have kept their alloys amazingly intact. 3M's product group dynamics (team approach) and decentralized autonomy (small, independent business units) continue to produce innovation after innovation, but never in fields 3M knows

nothing about. There seems to be little or no temptation at 3M to dabble in strategies that would compromise the firm's operating style or depend upon expertise it lacks. By the same token, HP prizes its small, entrepreneurial atmosphere, one inspirited by a strategic imperative of product quality and innovation inside what could be an impossibly large corporate structure for less excellent companies. HP's ability to inculcate an entrepreneurial culture and apply its product quality strategy to new markets and products demonstrates the company's commitment to the strategy-culture alloy. Although no momentary opportunity ever leads HP to forsake its cultural values, it does demonstrate the ability to make fine adjustments to both strategy and culture—as it did in the personal computer market—provided modification remains within the fundamental framework.

Dayton Hudson has chalked up impressive successes with its Mervyn's Department Stores, Target Discount Stores, and B. Dalton Bookstores, and despite doubling its work force over the last five years, the company seems to have protected its strategy-culture alloy beautifully. However, the company will have to work even harder at it in the future if it doubles its work force again over the next five years and continues to see its competitors in the retail industry siphon off many of its best people.

FIVE RULES OF THUMB FOR MANAGING TYPE A ORGANIZATIONS

Even if your company currently enjoys Type A status, you will not find it easy staying there. To ensure long-term excellence, observe these five rules of thumb for managing Type A organizations.

1. Find your company's relative position. Depending on your company's relative position inside the Type A quadrant, you may need to pay slightly more attention to either strategy or culture. A company at point "x" will need to shore up its culture, a company at point "y" will need to focus on strategy, and a company at point "z" will want to enhance both simultaneously.

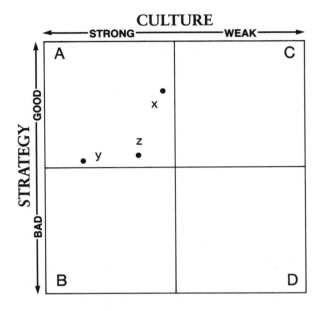

Citicorp might lie close to point "x" because it needs to make sure its culture remains strong during the transition from Wriston's leadership to that of Reed and while the bank invests heavily in its credit card business. Coca-Cola, in light of strategic vulnerability, may sit closer to point "y." And Dayton Hudson probably lies near point "z," where an equal emphasis on strategy and culture will be required in the growth years ahead.

2. Deal with strategy mistakes quickly. When you make a misjudgment in strategic direction, you must correct the problem immediately. Prompt recognition of strategic errors and swift action, regardless of any attendant embarrassment, will limit any damage to the strategy-culture alloy. Many executives like to think of themselves as infallible, especially after they have experienced Type A status for some time and forgotten that even the best executive makes mistakes. In fact, a lack of mistakes usually indicates a shortage of action—and inaction can hurt a company more than an honest, correctable mistake. The following graph represents the immediate resolution of strategy mistakes to remain in Type A territory.

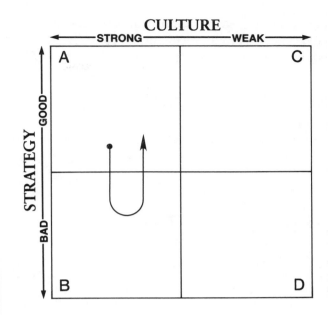

IBM's exit from the home computer market aptly illustrates how a Type A company should recognize and quickly deal with a strategy mistake. After introducing the PCjr in the latter half of 1983, IBM stuck with it for a while, making necessary upgrades in 1984, but then stopped producing the machine in the spring of 1985. It took courage to admit defeat and accept the fact that the home computer market and PCjr strategy did not make sense for IBM. Eastman Kodak, hoping to be in the right place at the right time when a new technology catches fire, has been dabbling in as many markets as possible: video gear, floppy disks, software that uses phone lines to make copier machines function like facsimile machines, blood analysis equipment, and more. Some observers have wondered whether Kodak has been pursuing a sufficiently unified strategy, without which it will almost inevitably lose its Type A status.

3. Resolve cultural inconsistencies before permanent damage occurs. Any strong culture can usually understand and tolerate inconsistencies for a short period of time. However, if a company has decided to consciously adjust its culture and has failed to clearly communicate an adjusted mission to its people (thereby justifying inconsistencies with the old culture as it transforms itself into a new one), lingering inconsistencies can cause permanent damage over time. Consistency resides at the very core of every strong culture and only speedy remedies can prevent long-range damage from occurring:

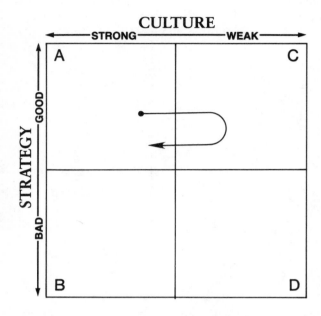

When all the world seemed to be telling Hewlett-Packard to change its decentralized, entrepreneurial organizational structure in order to compete effectively in the complex computer industry, HP didn't pay much attention. Although the company's management did undertake a reorganization to improve internal coordination and external competitiveness, it did not compromise "the HP way." That's why HP continues to attract some of the most talented people available. Merck, long considered the pharmaceutical industry's research powerhouse, experienced a drought in research around 1980 as the company's overriding commitment seemed to sputter. Today, however, Merck has brought all the company's resources to bear on regaining research dominance—in time, it hopes, to prevent any lasting cultural damage.

4. Strengthen your Type A status. Every company that currently enjoys a Type A position obviously wants to move deeper into Type A territory. No company can stand still and even the best must constantly strive for improvement. Improvement depends on managing both culture and strategy, though you can sometimes pay more attention to one or the other.

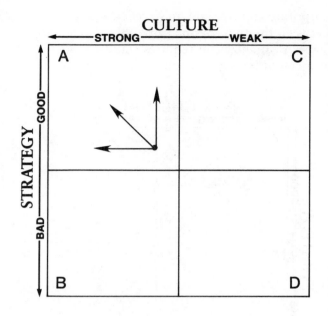

Marriott, known for its commitment to service, has not been resting on its laurels. Under the guiding hand of J. Willard Marriott, Jr., it has been moving in exciting new strategic directions while emphasizing even more its preoccupation with the highest-quality service. With its new Courtyard Hotels it hopes to tap the mid-price business traveler market; with All-Suite Hotels it plans to capture more of the upscale market; with Life-Care communities it intends to serve the elderly market; and with Time-Share Condominiums, it expects to carve a bigger slice of the vacation market.

Sometimes improving your position in Type A territory means saying no to an opportunity. Dow Jones turned down the chance for what could have been handsome royalties when it took legal action to prevent the Chicago Board of Trade from using the Dow Jones averages as a basis for index trading. Reputation and independent news and information are literally priceless to Dow Jones, and fiercely protecting these standards helps the company improve its position. It is not uncommon for Dow Jones to turn away millions of dollars in advertising revenues if it considers the advertised product or issue objectionable.

5. Devise strategy and build culture simultaneously. Remember, you only reach Type A status by having a brilliant strategy, a strong corporate culture, and an excellent match between the two. By the same token, remaining a Type A organization requires simultaneous strategic thinking and culture building.

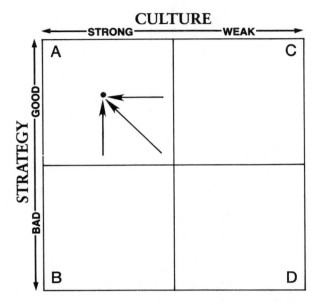

Boeing has hinged it strategies and culture on the commercial airline market, never getting sidetracked strategically by chasing military contracts the way its competitors have and never getting mired down culturally by falling prey to a bureaucratic structure the way others in the industry have. Marriott is improving its strategy-culture position by focusing on strategy while holding on to its strong service culture. Dow Jones is strengthening its strategy-culture alloy by solidifying its culture behind only those opportunities it finds compatible with the company's philosophy.

If you have achieved Type A status, practice these rules of thumb because only your dedicated vigilance can keep your organization in the ranks of the best-run companies.

ACTION PLANS

Bearing in mind the five rules of thumb for managing Type A organizations and the specific changes you considered in Chapter 7, you can now take action. In the next three exercises you will record your preliminary action plans, test them thoroughly with the Strategy-Culture Matching Grid, and then finalize the steps you will take to guarantee continued excellence.

EXERCISE 1
DEVELOPING PRELIMINARY ACTION PLANS

In Part A of this exercise you will summarize proposed modifications to your strategy-culture alloy. Seldom will you be making any sweeping changes, but you may be fine-tuning any one or even all six as you strive to solidify and enhance your position. Once you have identified and recorded all potential modifications, restate your strategy and culture if necessary. In Part B you will record specific steps you could take to implement any modifications.

Let's return to our newspaper example from Chapter 3. From the Introduction to Part II you will recall that the newspaper's strategy and culture rankings placed it in the Type A quadrant. Although the firm enjoyed a strong strategy and culture position, it still felt it should make some modifications to prepare itself for future growth and expansion into related fields. The newspaper's management team filled out Part A of Exercise 1 in the following way:

EXERCISE 1 EXAMPLE, PART A

---

1. Strategy

A. **Proposed modifications in the way your company satisfies customer needs:** *No change.*

B. **Proposed modifications in the way your company sustains competitive advantage:** *Our competitive advantage is innovation in all aspects of journalism, for our current markets and new ones we expect to enter. In order to sustain that advantage we must remain as close to the leading edge in new approaches to journalism as possible, while at the same time holding our reputation for good reporting intact. This means we need to institutionalize our innovativeness more than we have in the past, especially as we apply our innovativeness to new markets and businesses.*

C. **Proposed modifications in the way your company capitalizes on company strengths:** *No change.*

Restate your company's strategy incorporating the above modifications: *It is our strategy to build upon our success in reputable, innovative journalism by moving into similar and related markets. We expect the institutionalization of innovative approaches will allow us to penetrate new markets easily, but to continue growing in individual markets we must maintain high standards of quality as well.*

2. Culture

D. **Proposed modifications in the way your company cultivates commitment to a common purpose:** *Our commitment originally rested on superior journalism, then shifted to innovation in the presentation of news. For the future we must carefully blend these two purposes to create a new commitment to a reputation for superior journalism presented in innovative ways.*

E. **Proposed modifications in the way your company sustains competitive advantage:** *No change.*

F. **Proposed modifications in the way your company maintains consistency in perpetuating commitment and competence:** *No change.*

Redescribe your company's culture incorporating the above modifications: *Our company's culture is committed to superior journalism presented in innovative ways, backed by our competence to innovate and sustained by our unyielding consistency.*

As you proceed with this exercise, try to write something more than "No change" under each strategy-culture component. Even if you do not plan an immediate change in one area, you may be able to imagine a future situation that would demand some action. You can label such possibilities "potential changes" and file them for later review and consideration.

EXERCISE 1 WORKSHEET, PART A

Developing Preliminary ActionPlans

1. Strategy

A. Proposed modifications in the way your company satisfies customer needs: _____

_____
_____
_____
_____
_____
_____
_____

B. Proposed modifications in the way your company sustains competitive advantage: ___

_____
_____
_____
_____
_____
_____
_____

C. Proposed modifications in the way your company capitalizes on company strengths: _

_____
_____
_____
_____
_____
_____

Restate your company's strategy incorporating the above modifications: _____

_____
_____
_____
_____
_____
_____

2. Culture

D. Proposed modifications in the way your company cultivates commitment to a common purpose: _____

_____
_____
_____
_____
_____
_____
_____

E. Proposed modifications in the way your company develops competence to deliver superior performance: _____

_____
_____
_____
_____
_____
_____

F. Proposed modifications in the way your company maintains consistency in perpetuating commitment and competence: _

_____
_____
_____
_____
_____
_____

Redescribe your company's culture incorporating the above modifications: _____

_____
_____
_____
_____
_____
_____
_____

The newspaper executives filled out the strategy portion of Part B in the following manner:

EXERCISE 1 EXAMPLE, PART B

1. Strategy

B. Steps to implement modifications in the way your company sustains competitive advantage:

First year:
Identify all areas within the organization where innovation is important and beneficial.

Develop a plan for institutionalizing innovation in each of the areas identified above. The goal of this plan will be to identify methods of encouraging and rewarding innovativeness among our people in the areas identified.

Identify all markets related to the communication of news and information that we could potentially enter in the next five to ten years and would benefit from our institutionalized approach to innovation in journalism.

Develop a corporate growth plan that schedules our entry into potential markets over the next five years.

Second and third years:
Monitor all efforts to institutionalize innovation in the key areas identified and measure results.

Finalize at least one major acquisition or merger.

Start at least one new business internally.

Fourth and fifth years:
Complete two major acquisitions.

Start another three businesses internally.

As with Part A, create change scenarios for all the factors, even if you plan to modify only one in the near future.

EXERCISE 1 WORKSHEET, PART B

1. Strategy

A. **Steps to implement modifications in the way your company satisfies customer needs:**

First year: _____
_____
_____
_____
_____
_____

Second and third years: _____
_____
_____
_____
_____
_____

Fourth and fifth years: _____
_____
_____
_____
_____
_____
_____

B. **Steps to implement modifications in the way your company sustains competitive advantage:**

First year: _____
_____
_____
_____
_____

Second and third years: _____
_____
_____
_____
_____
_____

Fourth and fifth years: _____
_____
_____
_____
_____
_____

C. **Steps to implement modifications in the way your company capitalizes on company strengths:**

First year: _____
_____
_____
_____
_____

Second and third years: _____
_____
_____
_____
_____

Fourth and fifth years: _____
_____
_____
_____
_____

2. Culture

D. **Steps to implement modifications in the way your company cultivates commitment to a common purpose:**

First year: _____
_____
_____
_____

Second and third years: _____
_____

EXERCISE 1 WORKSHEET, PART B (*Cont.*)

_____
_____
_____
_____

Fourth and fifth years: _____
_____
_____
_____
_____
_____

E. **Steps to implement modifications in the way your company develops competence to deliver superior performance:**

First year: _____
_____
_____
_____
_____
_____

Second and third years: _____
_____
_____
_____
_____
_____

Fourth and fifth years: _____
_____
_____
_____
_____
_____

F. **Steps to implement modifications in the way your company maintains consistency in perpetuating commitment and competence:**

First year: _____
_____
_____
_____

_____
_____

Second and third years: _____
_____
_____
_____
_____
_____

Fourth and fifth years: _____
_____
_____
_____
_____
_____
_____
_____

EXERCISE 2
APPLYING THE STRATEGY-CULTURE MATCHING GRID

Before you finalize any modifications, you will want to use the matching grid to test the matches among all the strategy and culture elements. Regardless of the number of factors you hope to improve, you should reevaluate all nine combinations to make sure every strategy component and every culture component continues to work in harmony. As usual, you will rate each combination from A to F, then explain the rationale behind each rating.

When the newspaper executives used the matching grid to test their modified strategy and culture, they found some interesting yet predictable results. The match between their modified way of sustaining advantage and the company's commitment to a common purpose did not perfectly match.

CULTURE

D. Commitment to
Quality and Innovation
in Journalism

E. _____
_____
_____

F. _____
_____
_____

STRATEGY

**A. Institutionalize
Innovativeness
and Exploit
It Through
Expansion**

1. Matching Grade:

C

B. _____
_____
_____

C. _____
_____
_____

Evaluation of Match

1. Match between A and D:

Grade: ___C___

Rationale: *An aggressive growth plan that includes new markets and new businesses will place an extra strain on institutionalizing the newspaper's innovativeness in journalism and its commitment to quality at a time when the company is still trying to figure out exactly how to effectively institutionalize what it already has. Too much change too soon can be destructive.*

As you have done before, use the grid as a creative tool, testing, retesting, and thoroughly weighing the ramifications of all changes, no matter how small. Even small changes in one factor can cause large problems in another.

Applying the Strategy-Culture Matching Grid

CULTURE

D. _____   E. _____   F. _____

STRATEGY

A. _____

1. *Matching Grade:* _____	**2.** *Matching Grade:* _____	**3.** *Matching Grade:* _____
4. *Matching Grade:* _____	**5.** *Matching Grade:* _____	**6.** *Matching Grade:* _____
7. *Matching Grade:* _____	**8.** *Matching Grade:* _____	**9.** *Matching Grade:* _____

B. _____

C. _____

Evaluation of Match

1. Match between A and D:

Grade _____   Rationale: _____

_____

_____

_____

2. Match between A and E:

Grade _____   Rationale: _____
_____
_____
_____

3. Match between A and F:

Grade _____   Rationale: _____
_____
_____
_____

4. Match between B and D:

Grade _____   Rationale: _____
_____
_____
_____

5. Match between B and E:

Grade _____   Rationale: _____
_____
_____
_____

6. Match between B and F:

Grade _____   Rationale: _____
_____
_____
_____

7. Match between C and D:

Grade _____   Rationale: _____
_____
_____
_____

EXERCISE 2 WORKSHEET (*Cont.*)

8. Match between C and E:

Grade _____   Rationale: _____
_____
_____
_____

9. Match between C and F:

Grade _____   Rationale: _____
_____
_____
_____

EXERCISE 3
FINALIZING ACTION PLANS

Once you have tested your preliminary modifications with the Strategy-Culture Matching Grid you should be ready to finalize your moves. The newspaper executives ended up adjusting their preliminary plans by giving themselves more time to institutionalize innovation in key areas of their company before they began aggressively expanding into new markets and businesses. They made no adjustments in the actual modifications they wanted to make, but they did reconsider the timing of them. Here's how they completed portions of Exercise 3.

EXERCISE 3 EXAMPLE, PART A

No changes in the preliminary plans.

EXERCISE 3 EXAMPLE, PART B

1. Strategy

B. Final steps to implement modifications related to sustaining competitive advantage:

First year:
No changes.

Second and third years:
Start one new business internally, but make no acquisitions.

Fourth and fifth years:
Make two major acquisitions, probably in the newspaper field rather than in other news and information fields.

Start two more businesses internally, preferably further removed from the newspaper field and extending into the telecommunications and television fields.

EXERCISE 3 WORKSHEET, PART A

Finalizing Action Plans

1. Strategy

A. Final modifications in the way your company satisfies customer needs: _____
_____
_____
_____
_____
_____
_____
_____

B. Final modifications in the way your company sustains competitive advantage: _____
_____
_____
_____
_____
_____
_____
_____

C. Final modifications in the way your company capitalizes on company strengths: _____
_____
_____
_____
_____
_____

Final statement of your company's strategy: _
_____
_____
_____
_____
_____
_____
_____
_____

2. Culture

E. Final modifications in the way your company cultivates commitment to its common purpose: _____
_____
_____
_____
_____
_____
_____

F. Final modifications in the way your company develops competence to deliver superior performance: _____
_____
_____
_____
_____
_____

F. Final modifications in the way your company maintains consistency in perpetuating commitment and competence: _____
_____
_____
_____
_____
_____

Final description of your company's culture: _____
_____
_____
_____
_____
_____
_____
_____

EXERCISE 3 WORKSHEET, PART B

Finalizing Action Plans

1. Strategy

A. **Final steps to implement changes related to satisfying customer needs:**

First year: _____

_____
_____
_____
_____
_____

Second and third years: _____

_____
_____
_____
_____
_____

Fourth and fifth years: _____

_____
_____
_____
_____
_____

B. **Final steps to implement modifications related to sustaining competitive advantage:**

First year: _____

_____
_____
_____
_____

Second and third years: _____

_____
_____
_____
_____

Fourth and fifth years: _____

_____
_____
_____
_____
_____
_____
_____

C. **Final steps to implement modifications related to capitalizing on company strengths:**

First year: _____

_____
_____
_____
_____

Second and third years: _____

_____
_____
_____
_____

Fourth and fifth years: _____

_____
_____
_____
_____

2. Culture

D. **Final steps to implement modifications related to cultivating commitment to a common purpose:**

First year: _____

_____
_____
_____
_____

Second and third years: _____

_____
_____

EXERCISE 3 WORKSHEET, PART B (*Cont.*)

_____
_____
_____

Fourth and fifth years: _____
_____
_____
_____
_____
_____

E. Final steps to implement modifications related to developing competence to deliver superior performance:

First year: _____
_____
_____
_____
_____
_____

Second and third years: _____
_____
_____
_____

Fourth and fifth years: _____
_____
_____
_____
_____

F. Final steps to implement modifications related to maintaining consistency in perpetuating commitment and competence:

First year: _____
_____
_____
_____

_____

Second and third years: _____
_____
_____
_____
_____

Fourth and fifth years: _____
_____
_____
_____
_____
_____

CONCLUSION

Given the inevitable and, in many cases, accelerating changes that will influence the quality of your organization, you must take care not to congratulate yourself for a position of excellence at the expense of the constant vigilance required to maintain or extend excellence. Regardless of the success you may be able to create using the principles and techniques presented in this book, you will want to reassess your organization as a regular habit, determining when and how to make all the necessary adjustments that will keep your company's strategies and cultural characteristics working together harmoniously.

EPILOGUE

In *The Sun Also Rises*, Ernest Hemingway recounts a conversation between two friends, one of whom recently went broke. Explaining his predicament, the bankrupt friend muses that it happened two ways—first gradually, then suddenly. Most executives could say the same about the ultimate failure of their businesses.

Today's organizations, large and small, have become so complex that working in them, and especially managing them, can be quite daunting: employee-management relations, unions, local and federal government regulations, the pressures of intense domestic and foreign competition, the rights of minorities and women, exploding technologies, and the sophisticated theories of consultants all make the business of management an intricate task. Faced with these intricacies, many executives retreat to managing one part of their organizations, stressing whatever areas they have mastered. Others defer responsibility to those above them, below them, or even outside their organizations. Either way, the results are the same—their companies decline gradually, then suddenly.

In this book we have tried to keep the complexity of modern management in mind while at the same time offering a simple framework and two graphic display techniques (The Strategy-Culture Matching Grid and the Organizational Classification Chart) for reducing potentially overwhelming details into a useful approach from which any conscientious executive can benefit. More than anything else, we have tried to stimulate *a way of thinking about management* and tools for translating that thinking into action.

Our way of thinking suggests that you always take into account both strategic and cultural implications whenever you evaluate your company's performance or whenever you must make a critical decision. Regardless of the issue you're confronting, you can always think about strategy in terms of three basic components (customers, competitors, and company strengths) and about culture in terms of three essential ingredientss (commitment, competence, and consistency). You can think about any business problem this way, whether you're addressing a need for higher assembly line productivity or launching a new product for a pharmaceutical giant, whether you're developing long-range strategies for a Fortune 500 firm or getting ready to patent a better flyswatter. It's a simple way of thinking that forces you to ask penetrating questions about your organization, but it also embraces a great deal of complexity because the interactions among the six strategic and cultural factors are so dynamic.

To help you grasp the rich possibilities of these ever-changing interactions, we invented the Strategy-Culture Matching Grid. This technique can make any problem, from the smallest hiring decision to the most global competitive question, more manageable, while at the same time putting the solution to the problem more easily within reach. Careful assessment should always precede any action, be it steps to cure bottom-line malaise or a plan for enhancing an already lucrative return on investment. However, throughout an assessment of your current situation or the likely effects of any proposed changes, you will always set your sights on eventual action.

Throughout this workbook you have seen examples of all sorts or organizations, from the desperately troubled to the perennially excellent. As you set about the task of leading your own company into the future, you might underline one word in your lexicon of management terms: *change*. In a fundamental sense this whole workbook has been about change: adapting to it, anticipating it, and even using it to invent the future. If you have learned how to make a wise assessment of your strategy-culture alloy, and if you have learned how to creatively use the tools supplied, you should now be in a position to harness your own destiny. Excellence really does lie within reach of anyone willing to invest the time and effort to get there.

For further information about
CREATING EXCELLENCE write to:

Management Perspectives Group
6925 Union Park Center, Suite 300
Midvale, Utah 84047
or call (801) 566-6736.